THE SIGNS SHALL FOLLOW

How *to* Activate *the* Spiritual Gifts Within You

by Aaron McMahon

THESE SIGNS SHALL FOLLOW
How to activate the spiritual gifts within you

Copyright © 2008 by Aaron McMahon
All rights reserved.

International Standard Book Number: 978-0-557-36686-6

This book is protected by the copyright law of the United States of America. This book may not be copied or reprinted for commercial gain or profit. The use of short quotations or occasional page copying for personal or group study is permitted and encouraged. Permission will be granted upon request.

Unless otherwise noted, all Scripture quotations are from the Holy Bible, New International Version. Copyright © 1973, 1978, 1984, International Bible Society. Used by permission of Zondervan. All rights reserved.

The "NIV" and "New International Version" trademarks are registered in the United States Patent and Trademark Office by International Bible Society. Use of either trademark requires the permission of International Bible Society.

Scripture quotations marked NAS are from the New American Standard Bible. Copyright © 1960, 1962, 1963, 1968, 1971, 1972, 1973, 1975, 1977 by the Lockman Foundation. Used by permission.

Scripture quotations marked NKJV are from the New King James Version. Copyright © 1982 by Thomas Nelson, Inc. Used by permission. All rights reserved.

Scripture quotations marked (CEV) are from the Contemporary English Version Copyright © 1991, 1992, 1995 by American Bible Society, Used by Permission.

Published by Aaron McMahon

To place a book order or for quantity discounts,
please visit the author's website:
www.aaronmcmahon.com

Printed in the United States of America

Dedication

I dedicate this book to my parents, Richard and Gail, whose constant encouragement and support has helped me achieve impossible dreams all of my life.

I also dedicate this book to my brother, Nathan McMahon, not just because he also has believed I can accomplish anything I set my mind to, but also because he is genuinely surprised when I fail to live up to his belief. His expectations have always encouraged me in ways that words cannot.

Acknowledgements

I am extremely grateful to Bethel Church's passion and commitment to five things: revival, desperate pursuit of God's presence, the supernatural lifestyle, empowerment, and training-up/sending-out. I am also grateful to the two years of training I have received at Bethel School of Supernatural Ministry (BSSM). I thank all of my teachers who have poured so much into me and helped me to become the man of God I now am. Describing my incredible experiences at this school could only be accomplished in the pages of a book devoted to the subject (and perhaps one day I will).

The students at BSSM have become more than friends, they are now family. We've gone through fires and trials which have bonded us together as one body of Christ. I love you guys more than I can possibly describe. I am inspired by your passion, your pursuit, your hunger and desperation, and your acts of faith. The risks you have taken have greatly inspired and challenged me.

I am honored to acknowledge my teachers and spiritual fathers, Bill Johnson and Kris Vallotton, senior pastor and associate pastor of Bethel Church. Your weekly input into our class did more than teach us, it showed us what it means to be a spiritual father to a generation of revivalists. By discipling us, you taught us how to be disciples. You showed us that we are to do more than teach a message; we must *become* the message. And most of all, by believing in us, you allowed us to realize that there is no barrier between us and our vision. For this, I am extremely grateful.

My most sincere thanks go to my business partner, Charley Haupt, who has supported my decision to go to ministry school and has sacrificed greatly to make room for my busy schedule. Charley, I appreciate you more than I can express. Thanks.

To my intern overseer, Kevin Dedmon, thanks for your mentoring, encouragement, and feedback in the writing and publishing process. Thank you also for pouring so much into me throughout my internship and giving me such great opportunities to grow in leadership and ministry.

Thank you also to Michael Skilleter, Micah Knox, Kimberly Partney, Andreas Fjellvang, Blake Healey and Yvonne Martinez for your input and feedback during the writing process.

Table of Contents

Chapter 1: Introduction 9

Chapter 2: The Foundation of Your Authority 19

Chapter 3: Who Do You Think You Are? 37

Chapter 4: Creating a Revival Culture 59

Chapter 5: Mystery, Hope, and the Cost of Faith 73

Chapter 6: Activation 91

Chapter 7: An Introduction to the Gifts 117

Chapter 8: Prophecy 133

Chapter 9: Words of Knowledge 155

Chapter 10: Healing 169

Chapter 11: Now Go! 201

Chapter 1

INTRODUCTION

I am not the pastor of a church. I'm not the leader of an internationally-renowned ministry. I'm not the son of a famous minister. And I'm not (yet) a prolific author.

It is for these reasons that I feel eminently qualified to write this book. I am you, the reader. I am somebody who has been a Christian all my life and I have been longing to see the supernatural power of the Holy Spirit flow through me in signs and wonders. I have at times felt embarrassed to be a Christian because I was aware that I was ineffectual and powerless. I honestly knew the power of God. I have had encounters with His power and his love, but I didn't know how to activate my faith so His power could flow through me.

I know the truth of what I write in this book because just a few years ago, I was a "Sunday Christian" who became desperate for something more than "church" and decided to do something to change it. The result has been literally miraculous. I am a walking testimony of what happens when anybody, not just a minister or somebody "called by God," decides to passionately pursue revival and the miraculous life to which we are destined.

In the last couple of years, God has taught me many things. He showed me where the "start" button is on the engine of the Holy Spirit. Then He dared me to press it. When I did, I realized that the same Holy Spirit at work in Jesus, in the apostles, and in revivalists such as John G. Lake and William Branham is now at work in me. This is the same Holy Spirit available to every believer. God doesn't play favorites. He gives all of us access to the same power, without limits. The only limitations are set by us, not Him.

For the first time in my life, starting approximately three years ago, I learned how to step out in faith and walk in the realm of the miraculous. God has honored my steps of faith and He has done many supernatural things through me. He has prophesied to other people through me. He has given me words of knowledge about people, so that I was able to know things about them I couldn't have possibly known except through an immediate divine revelation. He has healed hundreds of sick people as His power has flowed through my hands. He has cast out demons. He has freed people from the bondage of witchcraft. He has done great and wondrous things through me simply because I said, "God, use me! I want your gifts! I want your Holy Spirit to work through me. I believe your promises. Here I am, send me!" And He honored my request because He's always wanted to answer that prayer more than I wanted Him to. He had to wait until I became hungry and desperate for more of Him.

I don't just want to teach you what I know. I want to impart to you what I have become. In this book, I will challenge you and inspire you. I will encourage you. I want you to honestly believe that you can have the power of the Almighty God of heaven and earth alive in you, healing the sick, casting out demons, raising the dead, changing weather systems, breaking spirits of poverty, releasing God's identity, and transforming our culture through the power of the Holy Spirit.

By the time you finish this book, you will not just learn about the spiritual gifts available to you. These gifts will be *activated* in you. You will learn practical ways to prophesy over people. You will know the importance of creating a healthy revival culture. You will know how to release God's healing for the sick. You will truly understand the authority you carry as a "citizen of heaven". You will walk in your

Introduction

identity as a son or daughter of God. You will understand the power of your spoken words, to release divine power and to transform situations.

Most of all, you will understand how to take your faith and put it into action which will release miracles around you. The Holy Spirit enables you to do signs, wonders, and miracles so you can glorify the name of Jesus. Once you know the basic keys, you'll realize it's not as hard as you thought.

And finally, you will realize that Jesus *expects* believers to do miraculous things. A life of miracles is the *normal* Christian life! Having a hard time believing such a radical statement? Read on!

THE "AUDIENCE MEMBER" MENTALITY

I am 34 years old. I gave my heart to God when I was three. I've walked with God my whole life, but ever since I was a child I've always wanted the gift of healing. I've seen healing ministers in church and I've seen the power of God work through them. I thought it was one of the most amazing things I've ever seen. Watching someone be healed by the power and love of Jesus made me fall even more deeply in love with Him. I eagerly desired the gift of healing in my own life.

Unfortunately, I believed a lie. Somehow, I began to define the limits of my Christian growth by the fact that I was always in the "audience" when a healing minister was up front releasing God's healing into someone. I never saw another "audience" member with this gift. So I formed the (incorrect) conclusion that people in the pews couldn't have the gift of healing because they weren't ministers or pastors or somebody "important." I know it sounds simplistic and ridiculous. But I believed it without knowing it. I only realized this recently as I looked back on my life and saw the pattern in myself. I wonder how many other Christians have this accidental view of the gifts of the Spirit. "If God would just call me into 'ministry', then He would give me these amazing gifts… then He would place His power and authority on my life so I could see Him work miracles, signs and wonders through me, also."

In fact, about ten years ago I was talking with another church member and I told him that I'd wanted the gift of healing since I was very young. He looked at me with a smile and said, "Well, if God calls you into the healing ministry, then you'll get it." Amazingly, he was both 100% right and 100% wrong.

As you'll read in this book, *every* Christian is called into the healing ministry! The man who told me this statement meant that if God called me into a "healing ministry," then I could have the gift of healing. But I have been in "ministry" ever since I was filled with the Holy Spirit!

I remember praying for the sick occasionally throughout my Christian walk. When I say "occasionally," I mean once or twice a year. Honestly, I hated praying for the sick. Yes, I had sympathy for them. I knew God could heal them and I wanted to see them be healed. But I didn't believe God could heal them through me because I wasn't one of those healing ministers on stage. I was just another "audience member." Without thinking this consciously, I basically figured that there was a reason I was in the audience: because if I really did have a gift of healing, I wouldn't be in the "audience" anymore.

My level of faith restricted the power of God that wanted to flow through me. I didn't believe God's power could honestly flow through me. I didn't know my identity in God. I didn't know that He called me, and every other Christian, into an amazing destiny. I thought it was a destiny that only belonged to a very select few.

Up until the time I was 31 years old, I had prayed for a number of people who needed God's healing. But I never saw a single person healed. This is why I disliked being asked to pray for someone. I had such high hopes, but I was terribly frustrated. My spirit was drawing

INTRODUCTION

me into my Christian destiny (to manifest the raw power of God), but my logical mind kept telling me that "it must not be for me."

Finally in 2004, God sent a wake-up call. I drove nine hours from Seattle to attend a conference at Bethel Church in Redding, California. I heard senior pastor Bill Johnson speak about the body of Christ's destiny. For the first time in my entire life, I heard a man of God tell me from the pulpit that every single Christian is destined to walk in power, healing the sick, raising the dead, casting out demons, having radical encounters with God, experiencing dreams and visions, and displaying God's power to the lost.

I sat there feeling stunned as I listened to this message. It seemed too good to be true. Was it really that simple? Sure enough, it was all right there in the Word of God. Once my eyes were opened to the truth, my destiny was set free.

About midway through this three-day conference, I went to the church's coffee shop called HeBrews. I'll pause a moment while you laugh. Okay. I had been to an ice cream shop several days before and I loved how when I put a tip into the tip jar, all of the staff sang a short little song of appreciation. I was joking with the girl named Liz at the HeBrews counter and said, "If I put a dollar in the tip jar, will you sing for me like they do at Cold Stone?" Without even pausing, she immediately replied, "No, but I'll prophesy over you for free." I thought she was joking. But I could see from the look on her face that she was completely serious. So I said, "Uh... okay!"

She never closed her eyes. She never put her hands on my head (she was behind the counter). She simply looked me in the eyes for about three seconds, then gave me one of the most amazing and specific prophetic words I'd gotten in a long time. And she just kept going. She gave me three very specific and accurate words. Some parts were new and other parts were confirmations but with extra details.

I walked back to my seat in the auditorium shaking my head in amazement. I thought, "How could a coffee girl give me such an amazing prophetic word? She's good enough to be doing this in front of the church! Why do they have her working in the coffee bar?" And it was at that moment that I realized… Bethel Church doesn't just preach the message that "everyone can do the stuff." They *live* the message. If everybody in the church can prophesy as well as anyone who stands at the front of the church and calls people out, then that means they can be anywhere. The girl at the coffee shop. The greeter at the door. The mom and dad bringing their three children to church. The janitor vacuuming the carpet. Everyone lives with the knowledge that they're all called to prophesy. They're all called to heal the sick. They're all called to raise the dead. I realized that Bill Johnson's message wasn't just a message from the Word. It was a message of truth that was being lived out at this church.

I had not only heard the Word, I experienced it. I had an encounter with the truth that went beyond head knowledge. I had no reason to doubt the truth now. If Liz at the coffee shop could prophesy as well as anyone I've ever heard at the front of the church, then I could too. And if she could do it effortlessly, as part of her normal lifestyle, then I would do that also!

A year later, I enrolled in Bethel School of Supernatural Ministry as a First Year student. At that point in my life, I had never seen a sick person healed through my hands. Two weeks after school started, I did. My roommate Ben came into my room and said he had been having a headache all day. He asked me to release healing into his body. I was eager to try out what I'd been learning in ministry school and I wanted to see him healed, but I was scared that nothing would happen. Of course, I couldn't turn him down because that would be rude. And I was curious to see what God would do through me now that I knew He could work miracles through me. So I prayed for Ben. I put my hand on his head and I commanded the pain to go.

INTRODUCTION

I prayed and commanded for maybe 20 seconds. I ran out of words to say and I wasn't really sure anything was going to happen anyway, so I didn't want to belabor it needlessly. I asked him how he felt.

I was shocked when he said, "Oh, you didn't even need to pray! The moment you put your hand on my head, the pain disappeared instantly."

That statement blew a gigantic hole in my religious performance mentality! What did he mean, I didn't even have to pray? Was that possible? But then, I remembered that there were times that Jesus never said a word to someone who was healed through His power. It was simply a matter of faith. God honors our faith, not our prayers. Yes, our prayer can be an expression of faith, but sometimes it becomes a *replacement* for faith; a religious exercise without an honest expectation of a miracle.

When Ben asked me to pray for him, I had "head knowledge." I believed theoretically that God could heal Ben through me because I'd been taught this in ministry school and I'd seen the truth in God's Word. But I needed to actually try it out so that it would be pressed down deep into me and become "heart knowledge." I had to take a risk and try it out, despite the fact that I had never seen anyone get healed through me. By taking a risk based on what I believed to be true, God was able to let His power flow through my hands the moment I put them on Ben's forehead. My faith allowed my hands to become a conduit for God's power.

Another two weeks later, Ben came into my room saying he had back pain and he wanted to be healed. He confidently told me, "I know God's going to heal me through you because He already did it once before." I placed my hand on his back, took authority over the pain, and commanded it to leave him. Once again, God healed Ben through my hands and my faith. Now, with two healings, I was gaining incredible confidence. God really did want to heal people through me! I really could offer the power of Jesus to the world! You can imagine my sheer joy at the thought of walking with the power of God inside me, ready to release it into those in need.

"Oh, you need to hear from God? Let me tell you what God is saying to you right now! Let me describe the pleasure He feels toward you."

"You've had leg pain for several years? The God of heaven and earth lives inside me and He wants to heal you right now through my hands. Can I place my hands on your leg and release God's healing power into your body?"

I felt like my Christian life had just received a massive jolt of adrenaline. I felt more alive than I've ever felt in my life. Even as I write this two years later, I still feel alive. Every day is filled with excitement and awe as I wonder what amazing thing God will do through me next. I walk in realms of possibility where before I used to live in fear of impossibilities. Now, I *know* that impossibilities must bow before the name of Jesus. I know that I am His ambassador. I know that when I speak a word of healing, God's power rushes to that word to make it come true. I know that when I lay my hands on the sick, I'm actually laying the hands of Jesus on that person because He lives inside me and I am the body of Christ.

By understanding my identity, I walk with an expectation that people will encounter the God who lives inside me. I make room for Him to be seen in my life by taking risks and stepping out in faith. And I am seeing Jesus glorified as He works miracles, signs and wonders through me. He no longer walks on earth in His own body. Now, He walks on earth through my body. And through yours. And through every believer who is filled with His Holy Spirit.

I am no different than you. I am an "audience member" who encountered the truth of my Christian destiny. I am filled with the Holy Spirit so that I can glorify the name of Jesus by displaying his power to the world, just as Jesus did Himself.

Introduction

    This truth is for you, but it must be encountered through an experience. As you read this book, don't let it become mere "head knowledge." Look for ways to try it out. When you try it and you see that it works, then it will become "heart knowledge." You will have encountered the truth, as I did at the coffee counter, and you will realize that this is more than information. It is the reality of the kingdom of God.

Chapter 2

The Foundation *of* Your Authority

You were born for greatness! You were born with a destiny. You were given full access to the King and to the resources of His Kingdom, to accomplish great things. You were made to accomplish miracles, signs and wonders.

God is your greatest cheerleader. He wants you to do these things even more than *you* want to. He knows your heart, He knows you are desperate for more of Him, and that's all He needs. He isn't waiting for you to become perfect or holy. He'll help you take care of that along the way as you focus on Him and not yourself. Right now, He just wants you to move. To press into His kingdom. To press on toward the spiritual gifts and enter into the miraculous realm of Heaven. It's all waiting for you. God doesn't judge you as worthy or unworthy. If you have given your life to God, then you have already been made 100% worthy.

You have full access like a backstage pass. If you show a backstage pass to a security guard, they don't ask if you're passionate about the band or if you really, really want to see them. They just usher you in without a second thought.

Likewise, you have been given a backstage pass into the Kingdom of God. Everything there was made for you. While you are on earth, you are not only allowed to access it, God *requires* you to do so. It's not optional. He isn't waiting until you make yourself ready or holy enough, He is simply waiting for you to enter. The holiness will come in the process of entering.

In his book, *When Heaven Invades Earth*, Bill Johnson writes:

> Revival is not for the faint of heart. It brings fear to the complacent because of the risk it requires. The fearful often work against the move of God — sometimes to their death — all the while thinking they were working for Him. Deception says that the changes brought about by revival contradict the faith of their fathers. As a result, the God-given ability to create withers into the laborious task of preserving. The fearful become curators of museums, instead of builders of the Kingdom.[1]

We cannot allow fear to hold us back from our destiny any longer! Fear empowers our enemy, but faith empowers God. Often, He restrains His strength until we step out in faith. And then, He releases miracles. No more will fear rob us of our God-given calling. In the words of an amazing worship song, "The time has come to stand for what we believe in. Today, today, it's all or nothing!"[2] From this moment on, *it's all or nothing*. We've lived in our comfortable box long enough. And now God is saying, "Enough!" Jesus didn't die on the cross so we could stand around waiting until either the rapture or death takes us to heaven.

As Christians, we have an awesome destiny. We are called to be the body of Christ. Jesus walked on earth for a specific period of time, preaching the good news of the kingdom and demonstrating it through signs, miracles and wonders. Then, He went to heaven but He sent us His Holy Spirit to live within us. Why? So that *we* could become His body in the world, so that we could do the same things He did. In fact, He called us to do greater things than He did. This is our destiny. It is our commission as revivalists who have been called to bring revival to the world, to establish God's kingdom on earth as it already is in heaven.[3]

In the Beginning, Adam and Eve were created in the image of God. They were given dominion over the whole earth. They were given a commission: Be fruitful and multiply; fill the earth and subdue it. But Satan hated their identity as sons and daughters of God, so He began to sow deception into them. He wanted to take dominion over the earth but he had no power to do so. His only "power" is with the words and lies he uses to try and take what belongs to mankind.

With Adam and Eve, he sowed deception by telling them, "God knows when you eat of this fruit, your eyes will be opened and you will be like God."[4] He was trying to sell them an identity they already had! They were already made in God's image.

Satan's tactics are like some guy knocking on your door and offering to sell you a beautiful car that's sitting in front of your house... and then you do a double-take and realize he's trying to sell you your own car! Satan did the same thing by asking them to give up their identity in exchange for religion. Instead of having the authentic identity where they have dominion simply by being sons and daughters of God, he was offering them a religious mindset where they had to work for their identity by eating the fruit. When they believed his lie and ate, they earned the fruit of "working for their identity." They got religion (workers) where before they had relationship (sons).

Adam and Eve lost dominion over the earth as a result of their sin. The keys of authority over earth were given to Satan by mankind. But God still intended for mankind to have dominion over the earth, so He sent His Son to reclaim the keys of authority. Jesus fulfilled His commission and after His resurrection, He said to His disciples, "All authority in heaven and on earth has been given to me. Therefore *go...!*"[5] He had reclaimed all authority from Satan and He gave that authority back to His disciples. He told them, "Go into all the world and preach the good news to all creation. Whoever believes and is baptized will be saved... And these signs will accompany those who believe: In my name they will drive out demons; they will speak in new tongues; ... they will place their hands on sick people, and they will get well."[6] Then the disciples went out and preached everywhere, and the Lord worked with them and confirmed his word by the signs that accompanied it.

We are disciples of Jesus. We are to reproduce Himself in us, just as the original disciples did. We are called to the same radical, faith-filled, miraculous lifestyle that Jesus and His disciples had. The same Holy Spirit power that filled Jesus and His disciples is still available to us today. To believe anything less discredits the will of God, His commission to us, and the power He has made available to every one of us.

This is the normal Christian life: standing in line at a grocery store and noticing that the woman in front of you has a leg brace on. So you ask her what happened and she says she was dancing on stage as part of a school production and she accidentally fell off the stage, hurting her leg. So you ask if you can pray for her to be healed. She says yes. You ask if you can put your hands on her leg and she agrees. You kneel down, put your hands on her leg and you look at the leg, envisioning what is about to happen. For a split second, you can see inside her leg. You can see muscles, bone, tendons and ligaments. You can see the power of God in your hands like fire. You can see that you are transferring the healing power of the Holy Spirit that lives within you into the woman's legs as you touch her. This healing is occurring not through prayer or begging. It is occurring simply through faith and a strong belief in your own identity as a son or daughter of God. You know that the Holy Spirit's power that resides on and within you is like a car battery. When you plug a car battery into your car, all you have to do is connect the wires properly and you know that the power will flow. You don't need to stand there and try to talk the battery into being powerful or into releasing it's power. You just know it needs a connection. Your faith is your connection which is why you're kneeling on a concrete floor in a supermarket, surrounded by other curious bystanders as you release the healing power of God into the woman's leg.

You make some declarations of faith. "I command the muscles and ligaments in this leg to be restored and to be re-aligned properly, according to the will of God. I do not allow pain to remain in her leg any longer. I cast it out. And I release the presence of God to fill her entire body, to fill her leg, and to bring restoration and healing to anything that is physically wrong." That is all. No beseeching. No pleading. No "Please God, just heal her." Because you know that you are a co-laborer with the Holy Spirit and He is waiting for you to make declarations of faith so that His power can confirm your words, just as it happened with the disciples. They preached the word and God confirmed it with signs, miracles and wonders. You are a disciple with the same commission.

So you stand and ask the woman how her leg feels. And that's when you notice that her eyes are as big as dinner plates. She can only say, "I can't believe it! My leg has been in constant pain all day long and all of the sudden, when you put your hands on me and starting talking to it, I could actually feel the pain leaving my body. It was like the pain was pulled out of me... I could actually feel it leave! There's no pain left!" And then she's jumping up and down on her newly healed leg, praising and thanking God.

This is the normal Christian life. It is for everyone, not just "healing ministers" or pastors of mega-churches. It is for you. And the fact that you're reading this book right now tells me that you're going to be living this life. That's right, you will! First, you have to believe you can do it. Then you need to envision yourself doing it. Then you need to start doing it. After that comes the amazing testimonies.

I Cor. 4:20 says, "For the kingdom of God is not in word but in power." For the moment, forget the fact that you may not have seen any truly earth-shattering miracles. Just consider the miracles of the New Testament. Ponder the incredible miracles performed through the disciples. And remember that the word disciple simply means "one who follows and copies the lifestyle of a mentor." You are a disciple of Jesus. You are following and copying His lifestyle, just as His original disciples did. The kingdom of God is not in word but in power. Explosive, atomic, earth-shattering Holy Spirit power. If you have been baptized with an infilling of the Holy Spirit (and I hope you have!), then you have the exact same Holy Spirit power within you that was in Jesus and His disciples. Thus, you are called to the same lifestyle. To live below that call is to dishonor the power that lives inside of you.

The normal Christian life is one in which the power of the Holy Spirit is able to flow freely, rather than being locked inside ineffectual Christians who lack faith (as I used to be).

We are co-laborers with Christ. We are his disciples, learning to do as He did so He can replicate Himself in us. The whole reason He left earth was so He could give us the Holy Spirit which could work through us, reaching more people than Jesus alone could. He was the model, teaching us what we are to do. The gospel of Jesus was a gospel of power, miracles, signs, and wonders. If we call ourselves Christians, we must have no excuses for powerlessness. We have a high calling: manifest the raw power of God on earth. We are to passionately pursue the kingdom of God, seeking to establish it through the power of the Holy Spirit at work in us. Our Father is waiting for us to rise up and step into our destiny as the sons of God. If God's children won't do it, who else will? We have neglected our calling too long and believed Satan's deception that we are weak, powerless, and ineffectual. It has become a self-fulfilling belief which leads to less power which only reinforces it further. If we change our mindset and if we honestly believe the identity that God has given us, we will act on those beliefs and we will see God's promises come true. First, we must believe. Then we must act on those beliefs. Only then will we see God's glory manifest on earth through us.

The Moravians, a group of radical revivalists who prayed for 100 years straight for revival in the Czech Republic (and who received a radical revival), had an amazing motto: "Win for the Lamb the reward of His suffering." Jesus didn't just suffer and die so we could gain salvation. That was only the first stage! After salvation, we are now given a new identity as sons and daughters of God, called to establish God's kingdom on earth. We have been given the Holy Spirit so we have the power available to do exactly that. But the Holy Spirit limits His power to only as much as we're willing to risk through our faith. Want to see radical miracles? Have radical faith! Go search out testimonies of incredible miracles and then take ownership of them, believing that you have the exact same Holy Spirit in you which can repeat the exact same miracle through you. Then start to live it out. Soon, you'll have your own personal testimonies that will encourage and inspire others.

The Holy Spirit has given us gifts so that we can live and walk just as Jesus did. Jesus had the gift of prophecy, he had the gift of healing, he got many highly accurate and detailed words of knowledge for people. The Holy Spirit offers these same gifts to each of us.

I Cor. 1:7 says, "Therefore you do not lack any spiritual gift as you eagerly wait for our Lord Jesus Christ to be revealed." The gifts of the Spirit reveal Jesus in us to the world. If He lives in us but we don't express His power, then we haven't revealed Jesus. The gifts give us immediate access to the power of the Holy Spirit so that we can reveal Jesus to ourselves, to our families, to our co-workers, and to those we meet throughout the day. Jesus prophesied. The gift of prophecy reveals Jesus the prophet. Jesus healed the sick. The gift of healing reveals Jesus the healer.

We cannot reveal Jesus until we have the spiritual gifts He had which revealed Him as the Son of God. Since we have also been called sons of God, we must manifest the same power that worked in Jesus. This power at work in us is the Holy Spirit which, among other ways, manifests through spiritual gifts that He gives us. We have been called to be Jesus to the world because He lives inside of us and we are His body. All we need to do is ensure that we don't limit His power through doubt, wrong identity, or lack of faith. All of these limitations are addressed throughout this book.

Ushering In the Kingdom of God

The Kingdom of God has already been perfectly established in heaven. Jesus prayed, "Your kingdom come, your will be done on earth as it is in heaven." Jesus knew the Father's will: "bring My kingdom to earth!"

What is God's kingdom? It is divine health. It is prosperity and abundance. It is dominion over nature. It is walking in our godly identities, knowing who we are in God. It is kingdom authority. It is peace, justice, righteousness, love and joy. The kingdom of God is all good and nothing bad. God has no evil intentions toward us. He has no wrath for us. He pours out His wrath and judgment on sin, not us. Jesus took our sin out of our bodies so that the wrath and judgment that must come upon sin would do so when the sin is far removed from us. The reason God had to pour out judgments and wrath upon His people in the Old Testament is because they didn't have a way for their sins to be removed from their bodies. God pours out his judgment on sin, but their bodies happened to be in the way. We, living under a new covenant, no longer have to worry about God's judgment. He still judges sin. He still pours out wrath on it. But it happens far away from us, as far as the east is from the west. God only has eyes of affection and love toward us. He is our Heavenly Father who is our greatest cheerleader, wanting us to succeed even more than we do.

This is our King. This is His kingdom. We are called to establish His kingdom on earth, to bring justice to social situations that demand it. To re-align people with their loving heavenly Father. To cast out pain, sickness, disease, and death because none of that exists in heaven. To release supernatural abundance and prosperity on people, families, businesses, cities and nations. Heaven already has more than enough. We must begin to establish the kingdom of "more than enough," "divine health," and "encouraging personal words from God" on earth through our declarations of faith.

The gifts of the Spirit help us to usher in this awesome kingdom of God. The gift of healing allows us to bring heaven's "divine health" and lack of sickness, pain and disease into people on earth. When they are healed, then the kingdom of heaven has been expanded into their bodies. No pain or sickness can survive in the kingdom of heaven. When we reveal the encouraging personal words of God to a person through the gift of prophecy, we have just built up another person as we have given them an encounter with the Father. We have also released grace into them because God always accompanies His words with the power to make it happen. Grace is the power of heaven to bring change into people or situations. God's words, including words given in prophecy, are always accompanied by grace. In giving somebody a prophetic word, we have given them the grace to grow into the fulfillment of the word. We have established the kingdom of heaven in their mind and heart.

The gifts of the Spirit are the tools on our toolbelt. To live the normal Christian life, a lifestyle of constant miracles, we need every tool because we're going to come across many unique situations. If you only have a hammer on your toolbelt, you're going to have trouble unscrewing something or cleanly cutting a 2x4 in half. You need different tools for different jobs. But quite often, the tools of the spirit work together in interesting ways.

A few months ago, I was having lunch with some people after church. The girl sitting across from me was listening to me tell testimonies about some prophecies I'd given recently. She asked if I would prophesy over her. I agreed and allowed the Holy Spirit to reveal something to me. In a few seconds, I saw (in my imagination, as the Holy Spirit revealed it) an image of her making specific hand motions. As I watched this short movie, I realized that she resembled a traffic cop who was standing in the street directing traffic. I could see her motioning with one hand while the other one was pointing in different directions like I've seen traffic cops do. So I told her what I saw.

As I described this, her mouth opened and her jaw got lower and lower. Her eyes got really big and she said excitedly, "I had that exact dream last night! I didn't know it was a dream from God! What does it mean?"

I didn't realize she'd had that dream. I just accessed the gift of prophecy, but apparently I got a word of knowledge mixed in there. A word of knowledge is any information that can only be known about somebody through divine revelation. It is information about the present or past. For example, it can be possible to get a word of knowledge about things inside a person's home that you've never visited, or the names of their parents (assuming you don't already know their names). Here, I had just given her a word of knowledge thinking it was a prophecy. I thought I was going to use my hammer but instead God handed me my screwdriver because that's the tool that was needed first. Then, when she asked me what her dream meant, I didn't do "dream interpretation." I simply continued with the prophetic word that I had been giving her and asked the Holy Spirit to reveal to me what it meant. He told me that she had a gift of administration, she was very good at helping people to find their place in the church body, and that she was good at directing people in an orderly and productive way.

The gifts of the Spirit work together in very unique ways. You may think you're giving a prophecy only to find out you're giving a word of knowledge. Or you may think you're prophesying over somebody when in fact you're releasing the exact grace that someone needs to be healed in their body. When you're done prophesying, you may find that the person was just healed of arthritis! Yes, things like this do happen. These are the tools that are waiting to be used.

Go get them, put them into your toolbelt, and practice using them so you are ready in season and out of season. And then use these tools as part of your normal lifestyle. Don't just limit it to "ministry time" during a church service. Every day, wherever you go, whatever you're doing, you *are* ministry time!

Welcome to the normal Christian life.

WHY DON'T SIGNS FOLLOW BELIEVERS?

Signs, miracles and wonders did not cease with Jesus and the apostles. All throughout the last 2,000 years, there have always been faith-filled Christians who have been exercising the gifts of the Spirit and doing miracles, following in the footsteps of Jesus.

So why is it that today we seem to have fewer signs and wonders than in the New Testament? The early church had divine revelations that allowed them to walk in a greater fullness than the modern church has had. While we still have complete access to the power and authority of God, without a revelation of how to access it and how to release it, God's authority and power that resides within us may not be manifest as easily. Also, through religion, denominations, and church control, the Church began to lose the gifts, power, and hunger that released miracles.[7]

The modern church is becoming aware of her identity as the bride of Christ. She is being challenged to live up to her full potential. With this identity is coming the realization that she has a God-given responsibility to act a certain way, to represent the Kingdom of Heaven, to manifest God's glory and power on earth. This is causing the church to hunger for what has been missing for so long: the ability to manifest God's glory on earth. It is a supernatural, divine ability that is accessible to the church. The more the church has been experiencing miracles, the more the church has been realizing we can have miracles as a lifestyle instead of as a rare occurrence. In the kingdom of God, hunger begets greater hunger. Receiving more results in hungering for more. This is exactly what Jesus wants from His body.

What can we do to walk in greater manifestations of God's presence and power? For many of us, we have not because we ask not. We must know what we have legal access to, we must hunger for it, and we must pursue it until we have it. If we don't honestly believe that we can manifest God's raw power on earth, we won't pursue it which means we won't manifest it. First, we believe. Then we pursue by asking. Then we eagerly expect to receive it. Finally, we get it. It's a simple process but it's a key that will be repeated often in this book because it is so powerful.

Revelation from God through our intimacy with Him is one of the best ways to grow in manifestations. As God reveals Himself to us, whether through encounter experiences or healings or prophecies or financial/relational solutions, we can see what is considered "normal behavior" in the Kingdom of God. Many times, we believe that a miracle is a last resort from God for a people that have screwed things up so badly, they need something supernatural to correct things. In other words, some may believe that miracles just show that "God is breaking His own rules out of love". This is not true! God Himself is miraculous; He is supernatural. He can't help but be that way. He wants to be Himself around His people, but He needs room to do so. He realizes how polarizing and demanding the supernatural can be. Miracles demand a decision on the part of believers and unbelievers to permanently increase their faith and to change their thinking. God doesn't want to impose this on us unless we want it. Are you ready? As you position yourself by expecting and praying for the supernatural, you will set yourself up for encounters with God.

Revelation is designed to increase our hunger and build up our faith. As God reveals Himself to us, we see Him in ways that are new to us. We know Him more as He is, we're able to worship Him in spirit and in (greater) truth. This builds up our faith because we can now expect nothing less than what we now know to be true about God. Anything less will now be abnormal.

Faith creates an atmosphere where miracles happen. Jesus returned to his hometown to minister but was unable to do many miracles there because of their lack of faith. He could only lay his hands on a few sick people and heal them. He was amazed at their lack of faith.[8]

How Can God Give Me His Power If I Don't Have Perfect Character or Holiness?

God does want character, purity, integrity, and holiness from His people. But He can do this simultaneously as we are pursuing His kingdom on earth. Just before Jesus ascended into heaven, He told His disciples to "Go and wait in Jerusalem until I send you power from on high." Not long after, the disciples—who only days before had denied Jesus and were in hiding—were given the Holy Spirit which gave them power. Jesus knew that the Holy Spirit, working from the inside, would change them into great men of God who would be pure and holy. But they didn't need to wait until they were perfect or had great character. They were given the gift of the Holy Spirit even while they still had character flaws. God has always used flawed men and women to do His will (remember Jonah?). He never chooses someone based on who they are or what they're like now. But once He gives them access to His power and authority, He expects them to grow in maturity and character. Growth is a process. He doesn't expect it to happen overnight. He just wants you to push forward. The kingdom of God requires pursuit, it requires pushing, it is a process. As long as you are pursuing holiness as the Holy Spirit works in you, you're in God's will.

In the meantime, don't wait to pursue the power of the Holy Spirit. It is yours now if you want it. The only one who can prevent this power coming into and flowing out of you is you! It is your choice.

As you grow in maturity and holiness, and as you steward the gifts of the Spirit well, you can expect God to test you. But these tests are a good thing because the reward for passing the test is greater power and authority. God won't give you all of His power and authority because it would be irresponsible of Him. If you misuse an enormous amount of His power, you will be under far greater judgment than if He started you off with less. So He gives you a small amount at first. Then, with good stewardship, He gives you more.

You will start off with a certain measure of God's power flowing through you for signs, wonders and miracles. But always, He is wanting to give you so much more. Keep asking Him for a greater capacity to contain and release His power and authority. Keep seeking after purity and holiness. Allow the Holy Spirit to work in you. With purity comes presence, and with presence comes power.

THE OCCULT IS THE UNPAID BILLS OF THE CHURCH

The occult has real power. Psychics often get real, accurate information. God warns His church not to dabble in witchcraft and the occult, not because it's fake or deceptive, but because it's very real. This power comes from a deceptive source and is not used for God's glory which is why it is evil. Satan cannot create anything new, but he can copy that which already exists. God's gift for words of knowledge is distorted by the enemy and becomes psychic abilities. Any power the occult has is only because God made it available to anyone, expecting the saints to use it, but the law-breaker has stolen it to try and glorify himself.

Many Christians hear the word "trance" and immediately think "New Age" or "demonic." But we quickly forget that Peter was sent into a trance where he received a powerful vision. Trances are something God created for His people. God gives visions, words of knowledge, prophetic foretelling of the future, healing, instant transportation, even levitation! All of these were created by God, but have been distorted by the enemy. There are even some Christians who believe levitation is a demonic activity. And yet, how did Jesus rise up into the air at His ascension? He was levitated. How did Jesus and Peter walk on the water? They were levitating on the water. I believe angels are involved in the act of levitation, whether it is godly angels or fallen angels. This is possible because God has made it freely available to those who want it. But He wants it to be used for His glory.

Do you know why some police departments use psychics to help find missing children? Because it works. How do psychics do it, even though they're involved in witchcraft and displeasing God? They do it because they have a godly gift that is being used to further the plans of the enemy instead of glorifying God. If Christians were living on the edge, living a life of faith like we're supposed to be, police departments wouldn't be calling psychics for help. They would be calling Christians!

God has charged us with a purpose and a destiny: to manifest God's glory on earth, do His will, establish His kingdom, and display His raw power to the whole world.

When we step into our miraculous destiny, the world will stop looking funny at us and start looking *for* us.

THE NORMAL CHRISTIAN LIFE

Revivalist and healer John G. Lake said, "The life of the Christian, without the indwelling power of the Spirit in the heart, is a weariness to the flesh. It is an obedience to commandments and an endeavor to walk according to a pattern which you have no power to follow. The Christian life that is lived by the impulse of the Spirit of Christ within your soul becomes a joy, a power, and a glory."[9]

This "weariness to the flesh" perfectly describes my own pre-revival lifestyle. I was a Christian who longed for more of God's presence and power in my life. Yes, I had spiritual experiences. I got rocked by God during worship services. I had been knocked to the floor by the power of God on a number of occasions. I knew God was a God of power. But I didn't know how to release His power through me. I thought it only happened "if it was God's will." I didn't know that I had the ability to initiate encounters of power, for myself and others. I knew that God gave the gift of healing but I thought it only applied to a few specific people. I knew God gave people an incredible gift of prophecy… but only to a lucky few. I wanted more and I believed I could have more, but I didn't know how to access it. I didn't realize that I *must* have these things because my pattern is Jesus. I must look, walk, talk, and act just like Him because He lives in me.

I didn't know my identity in God. Once I learned it and believed it was true, everything else suddenly fell into place. Revelation results in transformation. When I knew who it was that God called me to be, I began to confidently pursue and acquire spiritual things that fit with that identity. And God could finally begin to grow in me the identity that He's always had for me. But first, I had to understand it. Then I had to become hungry for it. In Chapter 3, you will learn who you are.

---

[1] *When Heaven Invades Earth*, Bill Johnson, p. 177, Destiny Image Publishers

[2] "The Time Has Come", Hillsong United, http://www.hillsong.com

[3] The revelation that we, as Christians, are not to stand around looking up into the sky waiting for our Savior to return, and that we are in fact called to establish God's kingdom on earth is from Bill Johnson's teaching on the subject. I highly recommend his book, *When Heaven Invades Earth*,

available in most bookstores. My book uses that God-given revelation as a foundation, with only a cursory explanation to save space.

[4] Genesis 3:5

[5] Matthew 28:18-19

[6] Mark 16:15-18

[7] I recommend the book *2,000 Years of Charismatic Christianity* by Eddie L. Hyatt (available in most bookstores). The author traces an unbroken line of miracles, signs and wonders from the time of Jesus until today. Along the way, he shows the different periods during which the organized church began to shut down miracles, signs and wonders because people in power usually lacked them but the "church lay members" were still doing them. To avoid embarrassment, the organized church leaders began to "excommunicate" or even kill lay members who were doing miracles or healings. As a result, miracles began to be forced out of the church, starting around the 300's to 400's AD. This book is a must-read so we can know and learn from our own Christian history! It is fascinating and very easy to read.

[8] Matthew 13:58, Mark 6:5-6

[9] *John G. Lake: His Life, His Sermons, His Boldness of Faith*, Kenneth Copeland Publications, p. 249

Chapter 3

WHO DO YOU THINK YOU ARE?

Both heaven and hell are asking you one question, and both are eagerly waiting to know your answer: ***Who do you think you are?***

Heaven wants to know who you think you are so the Holy Spirit can equip you with the tools that fit with the revelation of your identity. Heaven is waiting to release things into you, but only if you believe that you are who God says you are. Are you a saint? Or are you a sinner saved by grace? Are you a servant of God? Or are you a friend of God?

Hell wants to know who you think you are. It is desperately trying to talk you out of your heavenly identity and kingdom authority so that you *won't* live a supernatural life of power through faith. Hell is terrified that you will find out who you really are.

Authority in the kingdom of God requires us to know our identity in God.

Right now, I want to you read the next couple of paragraphs very carefully. Then I want you to set this book down and actually do it. Don't think about doing it. Actually *do* it. You're not reading this book to be entertained, you're reading because you want to learn.

This is a powerful thing you're going to learn but it requires an action.

I want you to look at your hands closely. Turn them over, look at both sides. Notice every wrinkle and line, every blood vessel just under the skin. Now, I want you to say this out loud: "Jesus lives inside me. I am a temple and I am filled with His presence. I am also the body of Christ. That means these hands are the hands of Jesus. Every time I touch someone, it is the hands of Jesus that touches them. Every time I lay these hands on the sick, these are the hands of Jesus which release His power. Every time I hug someone with these hands or shake someone else's hand, they are encountering the physical body of Christ. The Holy Spirit lives in me, so I am the physical body of Jesus."

Jesus walked in bodily form for about 33 years while He was on earth. Then He died, was resurrected, walked around for another month or so, then ascended physically into heaven. But He left because He wanted to send you His Spirit, also known as the Holy Spirit. Now He lives inside you. You are now his physical body! Jesus couldn't walk the entire earth and spread the good news of the kingdom of God as a single man. He wanted to do that through you! So now that you are filled with the Holy Spirit, you have that call on your life. Jesus wants to do that exact same things He did on earth… through you. He wants to raise the dead through you. He wants to heal the sick through you. He wants you to lay your hands on a paralyzed person so that He can heal the person… through you. Even though your body now belongs to Him, He won't violate your will. He will only do as much as you allow Him to do through you. Jesus wants to do the same things through you that He did while He was on the earth… in fact, He wants to do even greater things now than He did back then! The only limitation is you. He allows His power to be restrained by your will.

Many people don't walk in their full identity as sons and daughters of God because they still believe they are servants. Jesus said in

John 15:15, "I no longer call you servants, because a servant does not know his master's business. Instead, I have called you friends, for everything that I learned from my Father I have made known to you." This is such a powerful key to our identity that I want you to read that out loud, not just once but a couple of times. Then just meditate on it for a moment. What an awesome privilege we have to be more than servants of the Most High God... He actually calls us friends!

But even more than friends, God calls us still one step closer to Himself. Galatians 4:7 says, "So you are no longer a slave but a son; and since you are a son, God has made you also an heir." We are sons and daughters of the King. What do we inherit? Everything that Jesus worked for.

Let's say you have a good friend who worked very hard all his life to acquire a great amount of wealth. Because you are his good friend, he has written you into his will. When he dies, you are now legally able to acquire everything listed in the will. All of the wealth that he worked for an entire lifetime to collect, you receive for free simply because of your relationship with him. In this same way, when Jesus died He gave us access to everything He had. That includes His power, His glory, His compassion, His justice, His peace, His joy... everything. But He didn't just die, He also was resurrected and ascended into heaven. He sent us His Holy Spirit to live inside of us so that we can have Him living in and working through us.

We are no longer slaves, we are sons (and daughters) of God. As sons, we are heirs. We have access to the incredible resources of heaven. We have access to angels. We have access to Holy Spirit *"dunamis"*[1] power that is so strong, a single drop (if it were physical) would be strong enough to either destroy or create an entire galaxy. With an inheritance like this, how could we possibly be content to live an ineffectual life of Christian boredom where the most exciting thing that happens is when the minister closes his Bible after a long sermon on Sunday morning? Instead, we could be healing the sick, raising the dead, cleansing the lepers, casting out demons, changing weather systems and other exciting things that God is waiting to do through His chosen people. He has given us the Holy Spirit as our inheritance, God living *within us*, so that He can work miracles *through us*, just as He did through Jesus. That is our identity. That is our purpose. And that is our destiny!

My friend, welcome to the authentic Christian life.

What Do "Believers" Believe?

We call ourselves "believers" because we acknowledge that we live by faith. But what do we really believe? If we look at the fruit of our Christian lives, we can discover it. I did so a few years ago and was embarassed to discover that what I really believed and what I *thought* I believed were two entirely different things.

I used to think I believed that God was good. But I also had to rationalize the apparent "failure" of prayer when some sick people weren't healed and they died. The only logical reason I could come up with is that God had the power to heal the sick, but He didn't always choose to do so. As a result, I obviously didn't believe that God was good all the time. This would be like believing that an earthly father was good, even if he refused to take his daughter to the hospital when she was sick with pneumonia. If an earthly father would care for his sick child, how much more does God want to care for His children? God is better than any earthly father could ever be. The key difference here is that He's given the responsibility, power and authority to *us*. If we don't bring the healing, it probably won't happen because He chooses to restrain Himself to whatever we're willing to do. That truth is both exciting and terrifying.

I used to believe that all of the Bible, especially the New Testament, was for me. But I later realized that couldn't be true because I wasn't *living* the New Testament. Obviously, I didn't really believe it. I didn't look at the lifestyle of Jesus and say, "That should be my lifestyle." I put Jesus on a very tall pedestal, safely out of reach where I could admire Him but thinking I could never really be like Him.

All of my actions came from my core beliefs. Strangely, those core beliefs can be different than our conscious beliefs. This is the difference between "head knowledge" and "heart knowledge."

Head knowledge is a fact that you know. Someone can teach you a fact and you will know it in your head. For example, if you had never eaten ice cream before, I could describe what it's like to eat Rocky Road ice cream. I would describe the texture of the ice cream, how cold it is in your mouth, the crunchy nuts, and the marshmallow crème. You could probably imagine this exquisite dessert in your head as I describe it to you. But the day that you actually eat Rocky Road ice cream for the first time in your life, your head knowledge will suddenly become heart knowledge. What you thought you knew will now be replaced by what you *really* know based on your own experience. To become a deep, core part of you, head knowledge must be experienced at some level. Then, you'll always know it through personal experience. Someone else's description of a truth probably won't change your reality. For that to happen, you must have a personal encounter with the truth.

My knowledge of God's promises in the Bible were head knowledge. They hadn't yet been challenged or tried, so they never got pressed down deep into my heart where I could stand firmly on them, never doubting the strength of their foundation. Trials are a great way to take head knowledge and press it down deep into our hearts. The first spoonful of cold, glistening ice cream with chunks of fudge, marshmallow and nuts is actually a trial. Yes, I know it's a difficult one but we must endure trials! The moment the ice cream touched your tongue for the first time, the trial pressed down the head knowledge into your circle of core experiences and beliefs, the part of your normal thinking that you will never again doubt. You will always understand, at a deep level, that Rocky Road ice cream is a gift sent from heaven, wrapped in sprinkles, and topped off not with a red bow, but with whipped cream and a cherry.

The miraculous lifestyle works the same way. If you don't have a history of seeing miraculous, powerful, supernatural things happen around you, you may have trouble believing it can even happen *through* you. Your head knowledge of miracles and the power of the Holy Spirit needs to experience a trial in which you actually *try* it out (that's why it's called a "try-al"). When you try it and see that it works, you change your mindset in such a way that it now becomes part of your core beliefs. No longer is the New Testament just a collection of amazing 2,000-year old stories and teaching… now it is a dessert menu, waiting for you to decide what to try next!

This has been my own transformation as I've pursued the supernatural lifestyle of ministry. I want to offer the world more than words. I want to offer them power. What used to be a set of interesting stories about Jesus and His disciples has now become my guidebook and my benchmark.

Now, I am starting to walk more in Paul's example which he states in Romans 15:18-19,

> *For I will not presume to speak of anything except what Christ has accomplished through me, resulting in the obedience of the Gentiles by* **word and deed**, *in the* **power of signs and wonders**, *in the power of the Spirit; so that from Jerusalem and round about as far as Illyricum I have* **fully preached the gospel** *of Christ. (NASB)*

Today, I can fully preach the gospel with both words *and* deeds, with the power of signs and wonders, by the power of the Holy Spirit who lives in me. I now have something to offer the world that is more than words. I have a supernatural ministry of power.

YOU ARE IN THE FULL-TIME MINISTRY

As soon as you get saved, you are in the full-time ministry. You may suck at it, but you can get better.

Jesus never intended for us to make church the only place people can get saved or healed. Jesus saved and healed the vast majority of people out in the streets, not in the temple. Many Christians think, "I need to bring my friend to church so she can be saved." No, that is what you are for! *You* are the minister. You are the healing evangelist for that person. You are their pastor. You are their teacher.

You are a revivalist. God has commissioned *you* to bring revival to the world. Maybe your world looks like your workplace. Maybe it looks like your neighbors, friends and family. Or maybe your world looks like all of Europe or Mexico. In whatever you're doing now, or in whatever you hope to do in the future, God has given you a commission in Matthew 10:8 when He tells you to:

> *Heal the sick, raise the dead, cleanse the lepers, cast out demons. Freely you have received, freely give.*

This is not a suggestion, it is a commandment. This is why you have the Holy Spirit. It's not just so you can speak in tongues! His power far exceeds the ability to give you a supernatural prayer language. The Holy Spirit living in you has the power to grow and restore an amputated arm in front of your eyes. He has the power to raise the dead through your verbal declaration of faith. He has the power to literally change the weather. He has the power to change the economies, politics, entertainment media, and hearts of entire nations. And He wants to do all of that *through you*. You are a revivalist, commissioned to bring revival to the world through whatever unique passions and dreams you have. God has called you to bring revival to your circle of influence, which is your "world."

By believing in your identity as a revivalist, you will start to live like one. You cannot become a great man or woman of God until you first believe you are great. Throw off all those lies of the enemy and believe in God's destiny for you. God is famous for using *anybody*, especially the least likely people who had no training. He used Paul, a man greatly feared because he was a Christian-killer! He used Peter, a man who could never say the right thing. He used Jacob, a notorious liar and cheat. If God can use these people, He can use anyone. All He needs is a willing person.

Do you know how the great revivalists of the past became revivalists? Granted, many of them weren't seeking to become revivalists like you are which is why it took them longer than it will take you. But they did have this: they were desperate for more of God's presence, not only in themselves, but also on earth. They wanted to see God manifest Himself in them and through them. They pursued the anointing and power of the Holy Spirit because they knew that when God does supernatural signs, wonders, and miracles, He manifests His face on earth. Ezekiel 39:29 says, "I will no longer hide my face from them, for I will pour out my Spirit on the house of Israel, declares the Sovereign Lord." The great revivalists of the past knew that when God pours out His Spirit, He is showing His face. So they passionately pursued the Spirit. They pursued the gifts of the Spirit. They pursued revival. God honored their passion, hunger, and willingness to "stand in the gap" by giving them revival.

You are a revivalist because you are pursuing more of God. You're pressing through to see Him face to face. And you will see His face as He pours out His Spirit on you and through you.

You're a Saint, Not a Sinner

All over the New Testament, the writers refer to churches and brethren as saints, such as when Paul writes to the "saints at Ephesus." He never refers to them as "the sinners saved by grace in Ephesus." Daniel chapter 7 verse 18 says, "But the saints of the Most High will receive the kingdom and will possess it forever—yes, for ever and ever."

We must believe that we are saints, because sinners don't receive and possess the kingdom. If we, as born-again Christians, believe we are still sinners, guess what? We will live from that identity. But if we believe we are saints, even though we don't feel like it or look like it just yet, our mindset and attitude will shift so that we *do become* saints. Our identity isn't based on who we seem to be now, it is based on who God says we are. God calls us saints. Okay, maybe we don't look like it just yet. But by living from that faith-filled identity, we open ourselves up to God's grace so that we can become what He calls us! On the other hand, if we consider ourselves sinners saved by grace, constantly returning to the problems that we always have, then we will be self-focused and sin-focused. We'll keep our eyes on ourselves instead of on God. He won't have any room to release His grace because we're obsessing over our own problems instead of turning our eyes to Him, believing His words of identity, and then eagerly expecting that identity to become true.

In I John 4:17, the apostle John wrote, "Love has been perfected among us in this: that we may have boldness in the day of judgment; because as He is, so are we in this world." We have boldness because we know our identity, we know we are in Christ, and the Holy Spirit lives inside us. Because of this, we know we can reflect Jesus to the world. The Holy Spirit is constantly working to perfect us "until we attain the measure of the stature of the fullness of Christ" (Eph. 4:13).

WE ARE WHO WE BELIEVE WE ARE

Christians have supernatural power to bring their beliefs, Godly or not, into existence.

If a Spirit-filled Christian woman believes that the Holy Spirit will never heal the sick through her hands, then her faith in that lie will empower it to become true to her. She won't pursue opportunities to learn. She will probably never pray for the sick, and if she ever has to (perhaps a desperate family member is begging her), she will probably do it with very little faith or expectation of healing. She might choose to find a "healing minister," somebody with the gift of healing, anyone else. She'll be afraid to take a risk for fear of not seeing the result everyone is hoping for. Her belief that she can't have the gift of healing will continually block her from accessing that reality.

Obviously, this mindset goes far beyond the gift of healing. My mother, for example, was a late-bloomer in school. She had some learning difficulties early on that made it difficult for her to keep up, so she was put into special education classes by well-meaning teachers. Through the expectations and actions of others, she was being trained to be a "special education" student. As a result, in social situations she was unable to use her brain rationally and she became unable to think for herself. Her thinking was very retarded and slow, so that she could not process things well or think things through. When she did try to do so, she "looked like an idiot" (in her own words). She stuttered. She didn't know the meaning of words. In short, she was being trained to be stupid through the expectations of those around her. What began as a simple learning difficulty, due to the unique and creative way that she views the world, actually caused her thinking to be impaired.

During the rest of her school years, especially in high school, she simply stopped trying. She couldn't function and couldn't think. She was, at times, suicidally depressed. She got by with grades that were just good enough for graduation, but she rarely gave any extra effort. After all, why bother? It would just be a waste of time, right? She'd never be good enough or intelligent enough. It was just easier to accept her "reality." She believed she couldn't learn, and that lie became true to her.

Luckily, she grew out of this crippling mentality throughout her twenties because she got closer to God and He began to renew her mind and show her that she *was* intelligent. He showed her the lie that she'd been believing. She accepted that He did create her to be unique, intelligent, and creative. She changed her mindset and started to believe God's new identity for her. When the lie stopped being true to her, she was able to discover and live in her God-given identity. Today, she is a talented painter and artist. She is an incredible teacher of the Word of God. And she is one of the most intelligent people I've ever known.

Perhaps you've heard someone say, "Oh, I'm just dumb," or "I'm terrible at math, you figure it out." You can see that they don't even try. This attitude becomes a problem if we apply it to our spiritual life because it blocks us from believing and growing in our identity in God. Once we accept a false identity, we build reinforcements (strongholds) around the mindset to give us a reason for our failures. "Oh, I prayed for someone once and he only got worse. God doesn't heal the sick through me." As long as you believe that, you're 100% right. God *won't* heal the sick through you. God values your will above almost all else. But He is eagerly waiting for you to rise up and cry out, "NO!! It's not okay that people aren't healed when I pray for them! I'm a follower of Jesus. If He healed the sick, then I'm going to heal the sick because He lives in me! There is *no good reason* why I shouldn't look like Jesus." Which mindset do you think requires more faith? Considering how our faith pleases God, which mindset do you think He is more likely to empower?

We need to be careful of the mindsets we believe. God has given us, His sons and daughters, divine power that can make our beliefs (whether true or false) become true. If I believe that a person I'm about to pray for will be healed, God's divine power is right there to empower my faith. On the other hand, if I believe that nobody will ever be healed through my hands, my faith has just empowered that lie. As Christian believers, we need to be extremely careful about the things we believe for this reason.

If we want to walk in power and be men and women of faith, we just need to believe that we can. We need to believe that our Father God is our greatest cheerleader who is eagerly waiting for us to rise up and take great risks in faith. We need to start believing every promise we read in the Bible. Then, we need to start taking action. Faith without works is dead. If we believe a promise from God is true, we need to act on it. We need to take risks. This is the kind of faith that shakes heaven and earth, causes revivals, changes people, cultures, cities, and nations, and which causes the world to sit up and take notice.

WE ARE ALSO WHO *OTHERS* BELIEVE WE ARE

When you were growing up, what titles or words were you called that not only stuck with you for many years, but defined your identity? These can be positive or negative. Perhaps your mom often referred to you as "the smartest one in the class" or your dad called you "Champ". Or maybe a kid at school called you a dork or a geek, or even something worse. These titles have a profound impact on who we believe we are. The people who we value the most are the ones who have the most impact on our identity. If you highly value your parents, you probably believe it when they say they're proud of you. But if you're chatting with the guy working behind the counter at Starbucks and you're telling him that you just got promoted at work, if he says he's proud of you, it probably sounds more like sarcasm or flattery. The exact same words have a different effect depending on who is saying them to you and how much you value the person speaking them.

But what about the words of identity that God speaks about us? After all, He created us! His opinion of us should be the supreme authority on who we believe we are. If we reject the true identity that He sees us as, we dishonor and insult our Creator. The more value we have for God, the greater His opinion of us will matter. The more we believe God's word, the more His words about us will become real to us. And the more we believe our identity in God, the more we will manifest our God-given identity in our lives.

GOD SAYS WE ARE:

Rather than just skimming through this list, spend a few minutes meditating on each truth. This is who God says you are. If any one of these truths feels uncomfortable or unknown to you, there may be a lie from the enemy in that area. Ask God to help you encounter each of these truths in your life so they will be more than words.

- **Disciples (followers and copiers) of Jesus**

    I John 4:17 – "As He is in this world, so are we."

- **Seated in heavenly places**

    Ephesians 2:6 – "God raised us up with Christ and **seated us with him in the heavenly places** in Christ Jesus."

- **Kings and queens**

    - Romans 5:17 – "Death ruled like a king because Adam had sinned. But that cannot compare with what Jesus Christ has done. God has been so kind to us, and he has accepted us because of Jesus. And so **we will live and rule like kings**." (CEV)

    - We are royalty. I Peter 2:9 – "**You are** a chosen people, a **royal** priesthood, a holy nation, a people belonging to God, that you may declare the praises of him who called you out of darkness into his wonderful light."

    - Jesus is known as the "King of *kings*." He gave us back the authority that was lost at the Fall of Man. Now, we are no longer slaves but adopted sons and daughters in His royal family.

    - We are made in God's image. God is the King and He expects us to live in His image as kings.

- **Sons and Daughters of God**

    Galatians 3:26 – "You are all sons of God through faith in Christ Jesus."

- **Co-laborers with God**

    - 1 Cor. 3:9 – "For we are God's fellow workers…"

    - Mark 16:20 – "And they went out and preached everywhere, while the Lord worked with them, and confirmed the word by the signs that followed it."

- **Children and heirs of God**

    Romans 8:17 – "Now if we are children, then we are heirs — heirs of God and co-heirs with Christ."

- **Citizens of heaven**

    - Phil. 3:20 – "Our citizenship is in heaven…"

    - With citizenship comes privileges and responsibilities: We gain protection from heaven, we have access to supernatural resources of heaven, and we are part of a powerful culture where impossibilities bow before the name of Jesus.

THE CHRISTIAN PURPOSE

We are called to do signs, wonders and miracles. It's our identity, responsibility and inheritance.

Jesus went about preaching the gospel and demonstrating that the kingdom of heaven was at hand. Everywhere he went, he preached the gospel and healed the sick.

St. Francis of Assisi, who lived a revivalist lifestyle, said, "Preach the gospel at all times. Use words if necessary."[2] Too many churches and Christians lack the power of the gospel which is demonstrated in signs and wonders. All they have left is the spoken Word. We need the *demonstrated* Word! The word of God is designed to bring us into an encounter with God. We don't just need to hear the Word, we need to become it! The world is desperate to know a God who demonstrates His love, power and compassion. They are tired of *hearing* about Him, now they want to *see* Him. Jesus didn't just come to earth to speak the word of God. He came to demonstrate the word, and to manifest God's heart of goodness through miraculous encounters. After Jesus ascended into heaven, the disciples "went out and preached everywhere, and the Lord worked with them and confirmed His word by the signs that accompanied it" (Mark 16:20).

As followers of Jesus, it is our duty and privilege to look like him, talk, act, walk, heal, pray, have compassion, and do miraculous works… just like He did. If we don't have this as our goal, we are living far below our destiny and the purpose that God has established for us. 1 John 4:17 plainly tells us that "as He is in the world, so are we."

The good news is that it isn't really that hard to do these things! There are a few key things we need to honestly know and believe in order to align ourselves with God's will. By becoming properly aligned, we put ourselves under his "faucet of anointing" out of which flows the power that we need to do the miraculous things Jesus did.

Key #1: Seek Intimacy With God

Seek His presence, seek His face, and be desperate for more — no matter how much of Him you already have, He is infinite! There is always more. Our hunger determines how much more of Him we attain. As soon as we become satisfied, we must stir up more hunger or we risk staying on that plateau. Many people aren't just staying on their plateau, they've built castles there. Meanwhile, more of God is waiting if we'll just continue climbing up Hunger Hill.

Our authority comes from our intimacy with God. As we pursue more of His presence, as we seek to know Him more personally, we begin to walk out our identity as "friends of God" instead of the former "servants or slaves of God." When we are friends of God, we talk to Him differently, we hear from Him differently, and we act differently. As we pursue God, we seek to create a dwelling place for Him.

Paul taught about this in I Corinthians 3:16,

> *Don't you know that you yourselves are God's temple and that God's Spirit lives in you?*

And he expanded on that in Ephesians 2:19-22 when he said,

> *Consequently, you are no longer foreigners and aliens, but fellow citizens with God's people and **members of God's household**, built on the foundation of the apostles and prophets, with Christ Jesus himself as the chief cornerstone. In him the whole building is joined together and rises to become a holy temple in the Lord. And in him you too are being built together to become **a dwelling in which God lives** by his Spirit.*

As we pursue more of God, we are also building a dwelling place for Him inside of us. We must expand our boundaries and push out the fear and mindsets that take up space where God wants to dwell.

In Bill Johnson's book, *The Supernatural Power of a Transformed Mind*, he writes,

> *If we understand and are confident in our identity as the House of God, we can do great exploits. No power of darkness in any realm of creation can stop our fellowship with the Father. There is an open heaven over each one of us, from the newest Christian to the most mature. Being the House of God means we have the exact authority Jesus has at the right hand of the Father. As a Christian at this very moment, you have absolute liberty and access to heaven.*[3]

Key #2: Expect Greater Things To Happen

If you expect the same things that have always been happening, the same things will keep happening. But if you expect greater things, you attract grace and power from heaven just like a magnet attracts steel. That's how miracles happen. Expectation produces faith and releases God's grace and power so that greater things *can* happen.

Jesus said in John 14:12,

> *I tell you the truth, anyone who has faith in me will do what I have been doing. He will do even greater things than these, because I am going to the Father.*

First, we must have faith that greater things will happen. Then, we must step out in faith by taking a risk. But we don't need to wait until "greater" things happen. Jesus also taught us to steward well what He gave us, whether it is 10 talents or only one. We may look at our one talent, then notice the person with 10 talents and say to ourselves, "I can't do anything with one talent! I need ten!" But Jesus commanded us to use whatever we've been given. As we use our measure of faith (whether it's great or small), God will increase it. And in fact, Jesus expects an increase because this shows that we've been using it. The more we put our faith to work, the more it will grow. Jesus will return one day and expects to "find faith on the earth," as He says in the parable of the persistent widow in Luke 18:1-8.

Key #3: Know Your Identity and Authority as a Son

If you believe you're only a servant of God, and not also a son or daughter of God, you're not going to have free access to the resources of heaven. If I go to my parent's house, I have full access to their television, their refrigerator, and their bathroom, all because I'm a son and I know I have that freedom. But if I worked as a plumber and I went to a client's house, I would have no right to dig through their refrigerator to make myself a sandwich because I'm only a servant.

If you're still living as a servant, you're missing out on the higher revelation that God wants you to live in. When you step into your greater identity as a son or daughter of God, your Heavenly Father can show you all the resources of heaven that belong to you because you've been adopted into His family. That means everything that belongs to the Father, everything that belongs to His Son Jesus becomes rightfully yours! All the power that Jesus had access to through the Holy Spirit, that same power becomes yours. As a son or daughter, you're expected to expand the kingdom because you are a prince or princess. In fact, Jesus is referred to as the "King of kings." Guess what? That means you're a king. You're a queen. You are "a **royal** priesthood, a holy nation."[4] Knowing your identity, and the authority that comes with it, will allow you to walk in that identity.

Key #4: We Work *From* God's Favor, Not *For* It

Unfortunately, too many people have a performance mentality. They are trying to earn God's favor, to earn His love, to earn His eye of affection. But we already have it! God can't love us any more or less than He already does. He loved us even before we first loved Him! That's why He sent His Son to save us, so that we could have a way to know Him intimately. If God already loves us this much, why are we trying to earn it? And God has also "seated us with Him in heavenly places."[5] Notice that we are *currently* seated in heavenly places now, not at some hazy distant point in our future. If we are already seated in heavenly places now, why are we trying to earn God's favor? We're sitting right next to the Father. If we try to earn anything from God, we're creating a religion that says "I have the power to get more from God by working for it." It's a selfish, performance-oriented mindset. We often get this from our own natural reality where the only way we can support a family, buy a car or house, or accomplish anything in life is to work for it. If we want to buy a television, we earn the money first so we can buy it. But we already know God gives good gifts to His children. Gifts aren't earned, they're free. If someone gives me an extravagant gift and I try to pay them back for it, they would feel dishonored and hurt. Jesus also said, "Freely you have received; freely give." If we're working for something we already have free access to, we're only going to see fruit that comes from the workings of man. But if we work from the favor of God that we already have, then we will see fruit that comes from God's power and He will be glorified, not man.

WE ARE ON THE OFFENSIVE, NOT THE DEFENSIVE

When Jesus visited His disciples after the resurrection, He told them he had taken back the keys of authority from the enemy and He gave all authority back to humanity. As of that moment, we are no longer on the defensive! If we believe Satan is stronger than us, it is only because we believe a lie. We have sided with deception instead of truth. God has given us power in our faith. If we put our faith into deception, it has the power to become true to us. So only by believing that Satan is more powerful than us can it actually be true. But if we recognize our identity in Christ, knowing that the Holy Spirit is alive within us, that we are citizens of heaven, co-laborers with God, and we have all authority in Christ Jesus, then we can walk with authority without worrying what the enemy is plotting. The gates of hell won't prevail against the church's offensive attacks. Let's act like we really believe it and start taking back the territory that is being defended by the enemy. We are on the winning team and we can't possibly lose. This is why I love being a son of God!

WHY DID JESUS DO MIRACLES?

Everywhere Jesus went, he preached the gospel and demonstrated the power of the gospel. He confirmed His word with signs and wonders. He didn't just talk and teach, he showed and demonstrated. The gospel is a message of more than words… it is a message of power. But power by itself is an invisible force. Power can only be seen if it causes a tangible change to something that we can see. In the case of Jesus, He most often used His power to heal the sick but he also prophesied, He gave very detailed words of knowledge, He levitated (when He ascended into heaven), He walked on water, he cast out demons, He changed the weather, and He caused food to multiply. He demonstrated that the kingdom of heaven was at hand. He didn't just tell people. He showed them. By doing miracles, He also revealed the kingdom of heaven to them. It is a kingdom of power, of justice, of divine health, of blessing and abundance, and of dominion over nature.

Miracles confirmed Jesus' identity as the Son of God. It's like a passport. Imagine you've traveled to a foreign country with a language that you speak without an accent. You can walk around this foreign country telling people, "Hey, I'm an American!" or "I'm Canadian!" and maybe some people will believe your words, but without an accent most would probably think you're a native.

Jesus was fully man (that is, without an accent) but God provided him with a passport that said, "The man who holds this passport is a citizen and an authorized representative of the kingdom of Heaven."

This passport is the Holy Spirit, who provides evidence through miracles, signs and wonders. The passport is what separated Jesus from everyone else, making it very clear that He was from a different place. Many people saw His passport and said, "Wow, there really is a place called heaven and Jesus is really from there. And obviously he was sent by his Father because he's got this incredible passport! Now I know He speaks the truth from God." Jesus was an ambassador, but now He calls us "ambassadors of reconciliation."[6] He has extended that title to His people. And He has given us the same passport: the Holy Spirit at work in us, doing signs, wonders and miracles with dunamis power.

Jesus commanded us to "Seek first the kingdom of God and His righteousness, and all these things will be added unto you."[7] Seeking God's kingdom requires two things: First, we must seek to be a part of it which requires salvation. Once we are adopted into the kingdom, we gain access to all the riches, resources, power and authority of the kingdom. We access this through the baptism of the Holy Spirit. Second, we must seek to establish and expand the kingdom of God in our own hearts, our homes, our businesses, our cities, and on earth. The kingdom of heaven wants to invade earth and bring its blessings and rewards. But it will only advance if *we* establish and expand it on earth as it already is in heaven.

Jesus also did miracles to confirm that He was sent by the Father. Miracles, signs, and wonders confirmed the identity of Jesus as a Son of God. Remember earlier in this chapter when I showed you in Galatians 4:7 that we are "no longer a slave, but a son." We, too, are also sons of God. Just as God confirmed the identity of His Son, He also confirms our identity as sons through miracles, signs and wonders.

Jesus said in John 10:25, "The miracles I do in my Father's name speak for me." And a little further down in verses 37 and 38, He says, "Do not believe me unless I do what my Father does. But if I do it, even though you do not believe me, believe the miracles, that you may know and understand that the Father is in me and I in the Father." Miracles build faith in people who want to believe in God. But people wouldn't want to buy a $50,000 car from you without first getting a test drive. Miracles provide the test drive and the "signs" that we do point the way to God.

We have an incredible identity as sons and daughters of God. We have been adopted by faith into royalty. As royalty, as kings and queens, we are called to expand the kingdom of God and to establish His rule on earth. It is only when we walk in our identity that we will begin to act like His sons and daughters, knowing that we have full and complete access to the resources of our Father's kingdom. Instead of begging Him for what we need, as a poor man or a servant might do, we know that we can ask Him confidently, knowing His only answer will be "Absolutely, my son. Go get what you need from my storehouses. Take as much as you want, it's all there for you to use."

This is our adopted family. This is our Heavenly Father. No longer are we called servants or slaves. Now, we are His sons and His daughters.

---

[1] *Dunamis* is the Greek word for "power," often used in the original Greek writings of the New Testament when referring to the power of the Holy Spirit (e.g., Luke 4:14-15). *Dunamis* is the root word from which we get the English word "dynamite," referring to the original meaning of *dunamis* which is "inherent power, ready to be activated and released." Believers who are filled with the Holy Spirit are also like dynamite: they are filled with *dunamis* which is ready to be activated and released by our faith.

[2] *The Westminster Collection of Christian Quotations*, Martin H. Manser, Westminster John Knox Press, p. 296

[3] *The Supernatural Power of a Transformed Mind*, Bill Johnson, Destiny Image Publishers, p. 59

[4] 1 Peter 2:9

[5] Ephesians 2:6

[6] 2 Corinthians 5:20

[7] Matthew 6:33

Chapter 4

Creating *a* Revival Culture

I've heard it said that you become like those you spend time with. If you want to learn how to become wealthy, it makes sense that you should hang around wealthy people so you learn to think like them, see opportunities like they do, be optimistic and passionate, and have a vision. You won't learn to be wealthy by hanging around the poor.

Culture works the same way. It changes others who come into it by the sheer force of inertia. If a person with a poverty mindset comes into a culture of people with a prosperity mindset, the subconscious culture that exists within the prosperous people will begin to change a person's poverty-mindset into one of prosperity, abundance, generosity and blessing. When enough like-minded people get together, there is a natural culture that exists among them. When someone with a different internal culture comes into their midst, their own culture will begin to change to reflect the culture around them.

The kingdom of heaven is the most powerful culture of all. It has the power to change anything that is willing. In the New Testament, it says, "Greater is He that is in you than he that is in the world."[1] If you have the culture of the kingdom of heaven in you, if you are passionately pursuing more of God, if you have great expectations for the miraculous to occur through you, then you have a culture that can change the internal culture of other people. In this case, it would be, "Greater is the culture in you than the culture that is in the world."

When you walk into a store where your spirit senses oppression, you have no reason to walk in fear because you know that the culture within you is greater than the culture of oppression. Simply by walking into a room, the atmosphere changes because you walk with greater power than anything else that exists in the world. Even if you don't know it, even if you never choose to use it, the spiritual realm knows and understands the power that exists within you. You are changing the atmosphere everywhere you walk, in every home you enter, in every store you walk into.

The power that lives inside you changes environments. I guarantee that every demon in a retail store or home knows when you walk in because they sensed an immediate change in the atmosphere. You may not realize it, but they suddenly became absolutely terrified. Their only hope is that you don't know the power you walk in so they won't be discovered and dealt with. The power of the Holy Spirit in you is the power of a transformative culture. Whether you're aware of it or not, this culture can change places, situations, and people around you.

If you and a group of others (whether it is family, friends, a home group, or an entire church) are passionately pursuing more of God, pursuing revival, seeking God's face, and pursuing greater miracles, then you are cultivating a powerful force that can change the culture around you. If only your home group is pursuing this because the rest of your church hasn't caught the vision, guess what? You are creating a culture among you that is so powerful, it can't help but change the culture around you! Soon, your church or other family members will naturally begin to grow in hunger, especially as they see the fruit of your pursuit. The culture of the kingdom of heaven is greater than anything on earth.

In this chapter, I'll give you some examples of how to purposely create a passionate revival culture and explain the effects that it will have. Knowing this, you can actively create a healthy culture in yourself or in your group that will allow revival to happen much faster, just as a tropical plant will thrive much more in a greenhouse than in cold open air.

THE IMPORTANCE OF YOUR SPOKEN WORDS

Our words not only reveal the culture in us, but they also change the one around us. If a father has a culture of fear and anger within him, he will speak often in anger which will change the atmosphere around him. Others will walk in fear when they're in his presence and they will feel powerless, so they will look for ways to take power over others, just as the father did. Likewise, if a father is extremely loving, gentle, kind, and generous, he will often encourage his family and give of himself however he can. He will speak words of love and kindness to them. He will be their greatest cheerleader, encouraging them to follow their dreams. He will inspire them to achieve even greater success. His words and actions reveal his own culture and they change the culture around him.

We must first ensure that the culture within us is godly and healthy. Then, we must speak it forth boldly. We must not let fear rob us of the opportunity to give an encouraging or loving word to someone. That may be the best thing a person has heard in weeks. Most of us have little idea how much life is in our words. God puts His power and grace on our words when we're speaking His words to others. I'm not just referring to God's words in the Bible. God wants to tell His people, "I love you," or "What an incredible job you're doing!" or "That was a great idea." When we speak those words to someone, God puts his power and grace on those words so they are a hundred times more effective.

God knows the power of spoken words. When He created the universe, He spoke things into existence with His words. He said, "Life and death are in the power of the tongue."[2] He has made us in His image so that we, too, have the power of life and death in the our tongues because His power lives inside us. We must be careful how we use it. We have the power to curse and the power to bless. Regardless of how we use it, there is an awesome power on our words. But the words of a saint are like a weapon: our words contain great power that can be used for good or evil, for construction or destruction, for increasing or decreasing, for building up or tearing down.

A prophetic culture is one of godly encouragement and building up of the body of Christ. Imagine that you've gotten a prophetic word for someone who is discouraged and you tell them, "I see you sitting in Father God's lap and He is whispering things to you. I see you listening intently, as a young child, and I see you giggling as He tells you secrets." Doesn't that speak of intimacy with the Father? Perhaps that person doesn't feel close to the Father at the moment. This is a prophetic word they're going to love to hear because regardless of how they feel at the moment, they have just been assured that they are close to God, they are in an intimate relationship with Him, and their spirit is joined with His. That kind of prophetic word builds people up. It creates a culture of edification, of strengthening, of love, and of unity.

We must use the power of our spoken words to create a culture that is edifying and healthy. Christians are not always operating at full capacity. Sometimes we feel oppressed, depressed, discouraged, frustrated or just plain tired. We need sustenance and encouragement from God. Yes, we can get it directly from Him. But it's even more amazing to have it come from somebody out of the blue. You don't have to go get it. God can bring it to you, if only someone is willing to spend a moment giving a prophetic word to you.

A prophetic culture goes beyond prophecy. It is one in which prophecy is allowed to flourish to the extent that it changes the cul-

Creating a Revival Culture

ture and brings on something new: divine love, honor, and seeing other people through God's eyes. Prophecy starts out by giving someone a prophetic word from God. If exercised so often that it becomes almost a habit, it changes your mindset in such a way that you often hear God's voice in every situation because you're so used to seeking and hearing His voice for other people. In doing so, you will see through God's eyes instead of your own. You see things from a heavenly perspective instead of an earthly one.

That person who used to irritate you, when viewed through the eyes of God, suddenly becomes a person you care about because God reveals the hurt and pain they're going through. Now, you have a heart of compassion for them because you've seen their pain and you are drawn to them. Before, you may have allowed yourself to be separated from them because they weren't meeting *your* needs by being peppy, outgoing, fun, and life-giving. But with the Spirit of God in you, showing you things through the gift of prophecy, you have life to give others. The life of God is magnetically attracted to those who need it. You will find yourself drawn to people who need what you can give. This is a healthy culture in which we pour into people, not because we're commanded to, but because we cannot help it. As we see people through the eyes of God, our godly compassion will draw us to people because we know we have life to give them.

This kind of culture is incredibly healthy for the body of Christ. It brings unity, strength, peace, and joy. By expressing and receiving love from other members of the body, a prophetic encouraging culture releases Holy Spirit "glue" that bonds the saints together in unity so that we become one body. It is an effortless bonding process because it is godly. When we try to unite together by pushing ourselves against other people, it will feel forced and awkward to everyone involved. But when we live in a prophetic culture, using our words to build up instead of tear down, we become united as one body with Christ as the head.

Pursue the Holy Spirit, Pursue the Gifts, and Pursue Greater Anointing

Passionately pursuing more of the Holy Spirit, pursuing the gifts of the Spirit, and pursuing greater anointing changes the culture in you and around you. The more you pursue, the more you acquire. And the more you acquire, the more hungry you are for even more. It isn't greed or selfishness, it is recognizing that God has given us the Holy Spirit without measure. The only measure is in us, not Him.

John 3:34 says, "For the one whom God has sent speaks the words of God, for God gives the Spirit without limit." Clearly, the only limit is us, not Him. He offers us unlimited amounts of the Spirit. The question is, how big is our water pitcher? I've ditched the pitcher and I'm just asking Him to fill an ocean within me. No matter how much I have, I know there is always more because the supply of God's spirit is infinite and without measure. As much as I have at the moment, I stir up hunger for even more. This is one of the secrets to growing in revival and in power. Learn to stir up hunger.

A Culture of Hunger and Desperation for More

Many things in the Kingdom of God are exactly opposite to the natural realm that we know so well. In the Kingdom, the first are last. If we want to be raised up, we must humble ourselves and go low before God. If we want more provision, we must give away what He has already given us. The hungrier we are for more of God, the more He gives us. But as He feeds us more, we need to ensure we don't become satisfied and complacent. We must stay hungry. In the kingdom of God, hunger must beget greater hunger.

Another secret to growing in revival is this: Be thankful for what God has given you already, then be hungry for more. Thankfulness produces increase. Before Jesus fed the multitudes with only a few loaves and fishes, He thanked God for the provision that He already had. Then as the disciples handed out the food, more was supernaturally provided.[3] Hunger and thankfulness are a powerful key to growing in God. We should always be thankful for what God gives us, but we should never be satisfied because there are no limits. That is how we stay hungry for more.

As you pursue God with hunger and desperation, as you pursue the gifts of the Holy Spirit, as you seek God's face and cultivate desperation to experience Him more in your life, you will reproduce this culture around you. Others will sense hunger on you, whether they know it or not.

Many times when I prophesy, I can immediately tell how hungry someone is for more of God. In one instance, the moment I sat down to prophesy over a young lady named Rachelle, I immediately sensed her incredible hunger. Because of this, it was very easy to prophesy to her. She had attracted prophetic revelation from God like a magnet. All I had to do, using the gift of prophecy, was open my spiritual eyes and tell her the good things that were hovering around her and sticking to her in the spiritual realm. Her hunger had attracted great favor and grace from God.

In another instance, as I was prophesying over a young man, I could feel a massive suction coming from deep within his spirit as if he was a powerful vacuum cleaner. I told him I could sense his incredible hunger and he was surprised I could feel it. I then proceeded to give him further prophetic words as God showed me how much He would honor this young man's hunger.

A culture of hunger affects everyone who comes into it. People who were complacent before will suddenly find themselves no longer being satisfied with the status quo. When they hear testimonies, no longer will it just be an interesting story that tickles the ears. Suddenly, a passion will burn within them as they realize they have to have that kind of testimony in their own life. Hunger begets hunger. It doesn't just reproduce itself within you. It reproduces itself in those around you. Find other hungry people. Form a group. Let all of your hunger, passion, and desperation feed upon itself as you seek God's face. God never turns away a hungry man. He always gives good gifts to those who ask.

As you begin to see an increase in yourself, others around you will also see it. The Holy Spirit will start to tempt them with the same thing, just like when you walk past a bakery and smell the aroma of freshly-baked bread. You weren't hungry a moment ago but suddenly you realize you're starving and you find yourself walking in… "just to check things out." And before you know it, you're walking out while eating a loaf of fresh banana bread and feeling extremely satisfied. Every time you walk past that bakery, even if you don't smell baking bread, you will still remember how amazing that banana bread was. And more likely than not, you'll stop in one more time. Hunger begets hunger. This is how a culture of hunger can change you and your environment.

A Culture of Generosity

Jesus instructed his disciples by telling them, "Freely you have received; freely give." Everything they had received, they were commanded to give away. We have received revelations from God. We are to give them away. Blessings? Give them away. Grace? Healing? Deliverance? Hope? Joy? Everything we have received, we are to give away to others who need them.

God doesn't just give good gifts to meet our own personal needs. He gives us more than enough for ourselves so that we can have enough to give to others. We are *not* to be the final recipients of His gifts. We are to be stewards, looking for those to whom we can give them. In the kingdom of heaven, whatever we give away doesn't actually leave us. There is no poverty in the kingdom. If I give away a healing I have received, I don't lose mine… but you gain yours. If I give you the joy I've received from the Holy Spirit, I don't lose the joy I had. But you gain joy.

To use a modern parable, I can compare the kingdom of God to a computer. If I email a picture to you, I still have that picture on my computer but now you also have a copy of that picture.

This principle is absolutely critical to a culture of revival. We must give away what God has given us. Then He will give us more. This is yet another key to increasing in blessing, grace, and anointing. Proverbs 11:24-25 tells us,

One man gives freely, yet gains even more; *another withholds unduly, but comes to poverty.*

A generous man will prosper; he who refreshes others will himself be refreshed.

As we give away what God has given us, not only will He replenish it in us, but He will also give us even more because we have been good stewards with what we first had. This is a key to kingdom increase. Want more anointing? Give away what you have to others. Want more dreams from God? Give the grace that God has given you for dreams to others who haven't had any prophetic dreams yet.

Everything that God has given us has come into us in one of two ways: Either directly from God, or indirectly from God through another person. We can get grace directly from God. Or we can get it from others who have His grace. We can get breakthrough by pressing into God. Or we can get it (often much quicker) by humbling ourselves and asking another to give us the grace from their own breakthrough.

The keys to kingdom generosity is humility and trust. I must trust that God is Jehovah-jireh — "God who provides." I must trust that I am His son or daughter and that I have free access to everything in His kingdom. I must trust that if I give freely, God will give me even more. But I must also humble myself and realize that God has given me things for others. If I have an anointing on my life for music, I should find ways to give that anointing to others. I can find mentoring opportunities to raise up others to do what I'm doing. I can't have the attitude, "God gave this to me, not you. Why should I give it away?"

We are the body of Christ, and the cells in the body need to replenish and support each other. We need to work together. Every cell in a physical body takes in and gives out. It takes in what it needs, produces something useful with it, then gives something useful out so that other cells can benefit. The body of Christ needs to work the same way.

The principle of giving away to others the spiritual blessings and grace that God has given us is referred to as "impartation." God imparts His grace to us. But we have the ability to impart grace to each other.

There was a student in my first year of ministry school who would often worship God with complete abandon. He would dance before the Lord in the most carefree way. Occasionally, I would notice him during the song service and I found myself distracted by his movements. As I watched him dancing freely, moving his arms about in time to the music, I would feel slightly embarassed for him. The embarassment came from imagining myself as him. I could barely imagine myself doing it but even that thought scared me!

So for most of the first year of ministry school, I felt only embarassment. I tried to keep my attitude pure and I tried to ignore his worship style because I genuinely knew that he was sincere before God. I knew God enjoyed his freedom of worship. And I also knew that my own flesh had a big problem with it. My spirit, on the other hand, began to crave that kind of freedom.

By the end of the school year, my spirit was becoming desperate for the same freedom he had. My flesh, however, was warring against my spirit. There was always the voice in the back of my head saying, "But look at him! He looks silly! I don't want to look like him.

Everyone will stare at me." Of course, I was probably the only one staring at him, but that only proved the point to the voice in my head.

Finally, as the end of the school year approached and I realized I may never see him again, I got tired of watching him and hungering for his freedom. I decided to do something about it.

I humbled myself. I mean, I *really* humbled myself. I had to scrape every last ounce of courage in me to approach him during the song service. I walked up to him and said, "I love the way you worship God so freely. I want to have the same freedom. Would you please impart to me the freedom you have?"

He agreed and he prayed a simple prayer of spiritual impartation. He gave me what he had. I walked back to my seat feeling exactly the same. I tried dancing and moving with the same freedom but still that annoying voice in the back of my head was telling me I looked silly, so I stopped.

Then, just a couple months later, I was worshipping God during a song service. I had forgotten about my desire to worship freely with my whole body, free of my internal voice of criticism. I had my hands raised to God as I sang with my eyes closed. And then I noticed, with my eyes still closed, that my hands and arms seemed to be moving. In fact, they were moving quite a bit. They were moving to the rhythm of the music. I opened my eyes and watched in awe as my hands traced beautiful patterns in the air. And then I realized that the voice of criticism that had ruled my mind during these moments was now absolutely silent. I looked around at the other people around me. Nobody was watching me. Nobody was pointing and whispering. The voice had been wrong! And even if people *had* noticed me, I wouldn't have cared because I had the freedom I desired! I had received an impartation through a fellow student, because of my hunger for freedom and my humility which conquered my pride.

Every person has grace that somebody else currently doesn't have. Look inside yourself and find it, then go find somebody who needs it.

Have you reached a breakthrough at some point in your past? Maybe you pressed into an incredible prayer life that took you beyond your initial boredom of prayer and reached a powerful level of communication and intimacy with your Father. You got grace from God to reach that level. Now you have grace you can give away so that someone else can have that exact same breakthrough! What may have taken you six months to acquire can now be given away instantly!

Wait a minute! Why would you want to give away something that you fought so hard for? After all, it took you six long months to reach that breakthrough, right? Why should another person get that for free?

Because "freely you have received... so freely give." You didn't earn the breakthrough. You just got so hungry for it that you pressed into it until you got it. And now, you have an inheritance that you can freely give away to others. And, according to Proverbs 11:24, the more you give it away, the more God will give you. Giving away what God has given you means you are simply being a good steward of what was originally His. Technically, you're not the owner... you're just managing a resource that still belongs to Him. As you steward and manage that resource well, according to His principles, He will honor you with even more.

The culture of generosity and impartation is one in which every member is giving and receiving from each other so that we can reach breakthroughs, receive grace, and reach new levels in an accelerated manner. Other people have grace for breakthroughs that you need. You can receive that grace from them directly and immediately through impartation. Or you can spend six months on your face before God. While there are times where the latter is the only method, don't be afraid to search out the grace that God has hidden away in others. He didn't hide that grace from you... He hid it in that person *for* you.

A Culture of Possibility

"With God, all things are possible."[4] How many times have we heard this or quoted it? Do we really believe it? If we do believe it, then we must act on it. Faith without works is dead!

Creating a culture of possibility is easy. Simply believe that every promise from God is true. Then act on it. Doing these two things begins to shift the atmosphere in yourself, in a group, in a church, and even in a city. Suddenly, things that seemed impossible to you seem possible when viewed through the "lens of possibility." These lenses are the vision of heaven. When God looks at us or at the earth, all He sees is possibility! He doesn't look at anything and say, "Whoa, now that's impossible." He doesn't look at a person's screwed-up life and say, "Man, there's nothing I can do with that poor sap. He's a goner." With God, all things are possible.

We must learn to see situations and people through the vision of heaven, through the eyes of God, through the lenses of possibility. As we begin to *see* all things as possible, then we'll begin to *act* on it. Wherever it was at first impossible for a paralyzed person to ever be able to walk again, when viewed through the lenses of possibility, suddenly you realize that if Jesus and His disciples could heal paralyzed men, this guy can be healed too! Then you can take action on that belief. Now it is possible. This will change not only your outlook, but also your actions.

A culture of possibility will change your prayer life. It will change your Christian walk. And even more, it will change the very atmosphere around you. When other people are around you, they'll notice that you often talk of impossible things as if they can really happen. At first, it will probably offend them because it goes against their beliefs. But those beliefs aren't based on the Word of God. You who are now keeping your eyes focused on heaven and looking at earth through the eyes of God, will now begin to speak and act as if all things are possible. When others around you hear you talking this way, they'll start to wonder about it also. But they'll also be watching you. As you take action on your beliefs, God will come through with miraculous signs and wonders. He will confirm His Word in your life. And others around you will take notice. Then they'll realize that, indeed, with God all things are possible! You've just created a culture of possibility. What started within you is now spreading to others. And from them, it will spread to even more.

The culture of heaven spreads outward because it is superior to any earthly culture. Too many people on earth live in a culture of oppression, despair, survivalist mentality, pessimism, sorrow, burden, and hopelessness. They *want* to believe that greater things are possible. You have free heavenly access to the realm of possibility, where impossibilities must bow before the name of Jesus. You are a walking sign and a wonder. You bring the kingdom of heaven wherever you go. Miracles happen in you, around you, and through you simply because it's your lifestyle. You don't *try* to be miraculous, you simply *are* because you act on your beliefs.

---

[1] I John 4:4

[2] Proverbs 18:21

[3] Matthew 14:13-21

[4] Matthew 19:26

Chapter 5

Mystery, Hope, *and the* Cost *of* Faith

Faith is the bridge between hope and the miracle.

In the summer of 2006, a friend invited me to pray for his father who was dying of cancer. I had never known anyone with cancer and this was the first time I'd seen a cancerous tumor. It was quite large and was coming out of his back. He only had weeks left to live. He'd been prayed for many times by elders and faith-filled people in the church. I honestly believed he would be healed and so did he. I spent three hours praying and releasing God's presence into the room and into his body.

Two weeks later, he died.

For the next week or two, I experienced many emotions. Confusion. A little anger. Great frustration. Some despair. Where were God's promises? Why had I been seeking after the gift of healing? I thought I had it all down. I thought I knew "the formula". I had faith for healing, I was sure it was going to happen. The Holy Spirit showed up in such great power that I actually got drunk in the Spirit for the first time and was barely able to stand up. I didn't expect that or even ask for it to happen. It just did. The joy of the Lord was very strong on me and it was being released through me into the man dying of cancer. He was experiencing it as the joy flowed through me. I also got a number of prophetic revelations, such as specific things to pray for and prophetic acts to perform, which we did.

And yet, after all that faith, action and divine confirmation, he still died.

You can understand why I would be confused. For several weeks, I was reeling. Why did he die? Were God's promises really true? Could I offer people hope when I can't guarantee they'll get what they're hoping for? Was I being fanatical in my beliefs or should I adjust my thinking to be more "realistic" and pragmatic?

Events like this demand a logical explanation. The mind thinks it understands things (such as a "formula" that should work), but God and the spiritual realm operate very differently. Because we don't know the mind of God fully and we don't understand everything about the spiritual realm, we can't expect to know everything about how things should work. We're operating on partial information. God designed it that way so we would need Him for the entire process. Not just for the actual act of divine healing, but even for divine revelations and wisdom during the process. But even still, what we think will happen and what we're hoping for may not occur. The miracle we're contending for may not be won. Why?

A revivalist needs to be okay with the question "Why?" going unanswered for a time. This is crucial.

If you try to answer this question too soon, you're going to search until you find an answer. *Any answer.* The answer may not come from God immediately. So if you don't get one from Him, the next one will probably be from your own natural, unrenewed mind. And that answer will quite probably be wrong!

Because people and churches have been uncomfortable with the question of "why" hanging over their heads, many have looked for and found an answer: "God doesn't do divine healing today." Or "It wasn't God's will to heal this man."

Are those real answers that God gave? Or did they originate in the mind of a person who is desperate to know why their hope was unfulfilled?

The logical mind demands an answer. You will need to have self-control over your mind so you can reply, "I don't know why. It's a mystery." If you can do that, you'll go a long way in the kingdom of God and your faith will be unstoppable.

It takes great humility to say, "I don't know the answer, but I still trust God. I still know that He is good all the time and I still believe His promises." Believing without knowing the answer, while appearing weak and foolish to the natural mind, actually reveals the true heart of faith in a revivalist.

THE GREAT BATTLE TO ADVANCE GOD'S KINGDOM

We are warriors in God's kingdom. We have been called to advance His territory, to reclaim it from darkness and return it to God. Yes, God could do this entirely by Himself but He has chosen to use us in this great role. But He has given us His power and authority so that we are empowered to fulfill this role.

In Luke 16:16, Jesus says the kingdom of God requires us to enter it "forcibly". We need to pursue it with great fervor and zeal, pushing into it and expanding the boundaries of the kingdom.

We have an enemy that used to have authority over the earth but Jesus won back that authority and returned it to us. We again have authority and dominion over the earth, as we used to before the Fall of Man. Now, we must go and reclaim the territory that is currently occupied by the enemy. We are to remove the enemy from every area and to establish the kingdom of Heaven. This is the fulfillment of Jesus' prayer, "Father, your kingdom come, your will be done, on earth as it already is in heaven." Heaven wants to invade earth. We are partners with heaven. We have been given a mandate and a commission: Establish the kingdom of heaven on earth for the glory of Jesus. He gets no glory if we sit around waiting until the rapture. Instead, as we "heal the sick, raise the dead, cleanse the lepers, cast out demons," we will bring great glory to the name of Jesus as we use the power He made available to us. Supernatural power brings glory to God because it is only available through Him. God wants us to use His power, as co-laborers and partners, to do His will on earth by establishing His kingdom in every heart, family, business, city, and nation.

THE NECESSITY OF FAITH

Faith chooses to believe God's word above the evidence of the senses, knowing natural circumstances are to be kept subject to the Word of God.[1]

We must set aside our natural mind which only believes in what it sees and what it has previously experienced. Faith requires a deliberate decision to believe something that is naturally impossible. The natural mind cannot comprehend faith. It will war against you which is why faith can be so difficult, especially in our Western modern culture where we have technology, science, and doctors. Our modern self-reliant society seems to have little need for faith. This is why poorer cultures such as Central and South America and Africa have such great healings occurring. Because they are so poor, they can't afford to go to a hospital or to see a doctor. All they can afford is a witch doctor. They have seen the power of witch doctors to heal (through the power of Satan) and they believe in the power of spiritual healing. Unfortunately, they don't realize the terrible cost of witchcraft and the many problems that come with that healing. But they do understand the power of spiritual healing.

I have had the opportunity to pray for the sick in Mexico several times and was amazed at how much faster it is to release healing into them than in the United States. Their faith is already expecting a healing miracle because they know it is their only hope and they have seen it work. They don't even think for a second that nothing will happen. As a result, I saw about 98% of the people I prayed for healed in less than three minutes, with most miracles occurring in less than one minute!

In fact, on our mission trip in Tepic, Mexico, a student named Justin and I were wondering how quickly we could see people get healed. We noticed how little time it seemed to take and we realized we were probably taking longer than was really necessary. We decided to try seeing how fast we could get someone healed. We got it down to about four or five seconds! That really built up our faith as we realized we were living out the gospels and the book of Acts. And it tore down our religious thinking when we realized that we didn't need to strive for a miracle by praying longer or louder.

We were able to release these healings in such a short time because everyone's faith (the ministers and the recipients) was so high. Our combined faith was like gasoline and we had more than enough to release God's grace and reach the miracle quickly.

Those of us living in modern, rich societies have much to learn from our neighbors. We need to be so hungry for the miraculous that we ignore the "logic" of our natural mind, set it aside, and choose strongly to believe in God's promises. If we are in great doubt, or if we actively disbelieve (as some Christians unfortunately do), then we have just found one important reason for the lack of miracles in our lives.

Some readers may wonder, "Can someone be healed even if they don't have enough faith?" Absolutely! Jesus healed a man's son, even though the man had very little faith. He even said, "I do believe; help me overcome my unbelief!"[2] Faith is required to access the healing grace that is waiting in heaven. Most people accessed that healing grace in Jesus because of *His* faith. But a few accessed that healing grace *only* because of their own faith. The woman who struggled through the crowd to reach out and touch the hem of Jesus's garment was not healed because Jesus healed her. Jesus was surprised at her because He didn't know she was sneaking up on Him, but He was aware that healing grace had just flowed out of Him. When He saw her, he said, "Daughter, your faith has healed you."[3]

Faith is the bridge between hope and a miracle. We, as healing ministers, need to build up our faith because—for the most part—our faith is the only thing that will build the bridge between another person and their miracle. When I'm releasing someone's healing, my faith is usually greater than theirs. And that's fine because I'm ministering out of love and compassion. I will build a bridge out of my faith so that they can receive their healing. But occasionally, I've ministered to someone whose faith for their own healing is actually *greater* than mine and I got to watch them be healed. They built their own faith bridge and I got to see the healing cross that bridge and transform their body in an instant.

WE MUST BURN OUR LISTS

What do we do with previous attempts at radical faith that seemed to be spectacular failures? There is a strong temptation to keep a list of these failures as a reason to avoid walking in faith. With such a list, we can show it to God everytime our spirit goads us into action. We can instead say, "See, God, look at the times when I believed for a miracle and *nothing* happened! Why bother trying again?"

I'll confess that was my attitude for much of my Christian life. I'm still occasionally tempted by that thought when I attempt something risky and nothing happens. But honestly, I have no desire to return to it because God *has* been coming through for me now that I've abandoned myself to Him and to His power. I made a conscious decision two years ago: I told him, "God, I am willing to look stupid for you." And I meant it. The statement terrified me at the time because I knew there would be times that I would be standing there, exposed for all to see, having no explanation for why nothing just happened. But I also knew I had to abandon myself to God's promises and start acting on them. The rest was up to God.

As I acted out my faith and believed God's Word, He has done *incredible* miracles through me and through other people around me that are jaw-dropping. Sure, there are some times where nothing seems to happen. I can't explain them yet but I am asking Him for understanding because I want to know. I believe there is a reason and I know it has nothing to do with Him. I know He wants to do miraculous things far more than I want Him to. And I also realize that "our struggle is not against flesh and blood, but against the rulers, against the authorities, against the powers of this dark world and against the spiritual forces of evil in the heavenly realms."[4] There are unseen reasons behind those mysterious, supposed "failures." I cannot blame God because I know that He is good. Always. To believe anything else would greatly dishonor He who sent His own Son to die for me so that I could experience His love personally for eternity.

If we've had great "failures" of faith in the past, how do we avoid building a list against God? How do we keep our faith charged up instead of diminishing each time we step out and nothing seems to happen?

We must remember Paul's exhortation in Philippians 3:13,

> *Brothers, I do not consider myself yet to have taken hold of it. But one thing I do:* **Forgetting what is behind and straining toward what is ahead**, *I press on toward the goal to win the prize for which God has called me heavenward in Christ Jesus.*

We must forget what is behind and press on toward the goal ahead of us. The goal is "faith realized" in the form of heaven invading earth. All of heaven is waiting for us to bring it forth. The only thing preventing it from happening is our will. God values our wills so highly that He has allowed Himself to be restrained by our will. He will never violate our will. Because He values it so highly, He is always watching and waiting for us to allow Him to do miraculous things. *Our will* determines when and how it happens. God's will has nothing to do with it because it is *already* and *always* His will. We decide. That is a powerful statement. And it shows us how much God not only values our will, but how much He values us, His creation. He has restored us to our positions of authority, once again given dominion over the earth to subdue it and establish the garden of Eden, as it existed before the Fall of Man. Adam was given one command: extend the boundaries of the Garden so that the chaos that existed outside the boundaries would become ordered, beautiful, and a suitable place for God to dwell with men. We have once again been given that charge and that authority: to call heaven down onto earth, then to extend the boundaries until the entire earth is subdued and has become a suitable place for God to dwell among men. He has given us the power. But once again, as with Adam, it all rests on our will and our decisions.

To prevent our faith from diminishing if we have a few "failures," we can build up our faith by re-reading God's word to remember His promises. We can read about the great miracles of Jesus and the apostles. We can ask others for great testimonies that will build our faith. Listening to testimonies builds an expectancy of what is normal for the Christian life. They remind us that anything less, a Christian life without miracles, is *abnormal*. We may not yet know the reasons for supposed failures of faith, but we know who God is. And testimonies are a great way to remember how great He is! They help us to continue "pressing on toward the goal" of a supernaturally-charged miraculous lifestyle.

What do we do with our list of previous "failures" that we've been holding against God or against the lifestyle of faith? We must burn the list! We must absolve God of any supposed fault in those failures because we know that God is always good. He is better than we can possibly imagine because He is infinite and we can barely comprehend His amazing qualities. We know His heart for us.

Then we must do as Paul exhorts. We must strain toward our goal. That is the only way to win the race. Radical faith is what keeps us straining toward the finish line, forgetting all that is behind. Do we really believe God's Word and His promises? Do we really believe in His power? Do we really believe our identity and our destiny? Do we really believe the authority He has given us on earth?

If so, then we must walk in it. Because faith without works is dead.

RADICAL FAITH IS EXPENSIVE

Faith is costly. It demands risk. When we hope for something miraculous, when we go to God hungry and say, "God, I believe your promises are true, even though I have no proof in front of me, and I believe I will see people healed through your power," then God will do the miraculous through us. There may be an initial period where very little or nothing appears to be happening, but inside you, there is a great breaking down of old mental strongholds. Once those strongholds have been destroyed by your activated faith, then you will see an incredible breakthrough. I can promise this to you because God promises this! Either God's promises are true, or God is not God. As followers of Christ, we have a duty to stand on and believe those promises. We have a duty to not just believe them, but to act on them. That is radical faith. Yes, there is a cost. But there is a great reward for those willing to pay the cost.

In March of 2005, about 30 students from Bethel School of Supernatural Ministry went on a mission trip to Tijuana, Mexico. One day, they went to Revolution Street, the main tourist area in Tijuana, to set up an outdoor evangelistic crusade. The weather was very bad. It had been raining all day and showed no signs of quitting.

They began to unload equipment from the vans and, although concerned about the electronic equipment, setup the speakers and made sure to protect them from the rain.

There weren't a lot of people around due to the rain but that wasn't going to stop this team of passionate believers. They were here to serve the community by offering the kingdom of heaven. They were sticking it out, rain or no rain.

They got into a circle to pray and build their faith. They were here to work signs, wonders and miracles in people's lives. They were here to let the Holy Spirit work through them in great power. They were going to preach the gospel, and if necessary they would use words to do so.

As they prayed together passionately, the Holy Spirit's power came on them. Their faith began to build up like a pressure cooker. After a time, the group realized that anything could happen that day. Literally anything! One young man in the group remembered a dream in which he was in this same situation: he was in Tijuana to minister on the street, but the rain wouldn't stop. So, in the dream, he got up on stage and commanded the rain to stop and clouds to part. He believed God gave him that dream as a prophecy. He put his faith into action by taking a huge risk.

He got up on the stage, grabbed a microphone and started talking to the people who had gathered to see what was happening. He pointed at them and said, "How many of you want to know how much Jesus loves you?" A translator quickly grabbed another mike and began translating for him.

One or two raised their hands. He said again, "Do you want to know how much Jesus loves you? If you do, raise your hands!"

This time, more of them raised their hands. He was building hunger in them, getting them to be curious.

Filled with faith, he shouted into the mike, "Jesus loves you so much, He is going to do a miracle for you right in front of your eyes!"

Then he looked up into the gray cloudy sky. As raindrops streaked down his face, he shouted to the heavens, "In the name of Jesus, I command the rain to cease and the clouds to open up immediately."

And right there, before everyone's eyes, the rain stopped and the clouds opened up. A circle of blue sky appeared directly above them. Everywhere else in the sky, the gray rain clouds dominated except for the circle of blue.

For the rest of the day as they stayed and evangelized, the circle of blue sky remained, a testimony to a declaration of faith and God's glory. But all throughout the day and into the evening, the rest of the sky around them remained rainy. Several students went a few blocks away in different directions and discovered that yes, it really was still raining everywhere else. Theirs was the only location where the rain ceased.

Later that evening, when they were packing up their equipment, they loaded in the last piece into their vans and everyone climbed in. As soon as they started up the vans to drive away, everyone noticed that the rain started once again. They looked up into the sky and could no longer see the stars through the hole in the clouds. Once again, nature had dominion but they never forgot that they have God-given authority over nature.

Radical faith is expensive. This young man, and indeed every student on the team, was willing to take great risks because they believed in the power of the Almighty God. They knew their identity as sons and daughters of God. They knew their authority over nature, sickness, disease, and death. They decided to use it that day. I talked to many members of that team and they each told me that their collective faith was "through the roof." They said that any one of them had enough faith to run up onto the stage and do that, but only one of them had the idea to do it. He could have failed spectacularly. He knew it. But he was so intent on glorifying God with great power that He didn't care. He lived out the axiom, "Go big or go home."

He paid the price by being willing to look really embarrassed if nothing happened. He was perfectly willing for that to happen. All He wanted was to glorify God. And God came through because he paid the price for his radical faith.

The parable of the hidden field and the parable of the pearl of great price in Matthew 13:44-46 is a perfect analogy of the cost of faith:

> *The kingdom of heaven is like treasure hidden in a field. When a man found it, he hid it again, and then in his joy went and sold all he had and bought that field. Again, the kingdom of heaven is like a merchant looking for fine pearls. When he found one of great value, he went away and sold everything he had and bought it.*

Faith knows that there is a treasure waiting for us, but first we have to pay the price so we can find and claim the reward — the miraculous lifestyle available to us in the kingdom of heaven.

When Doubt Is No Longer Tolerated

When we have doubts, God gives us a grace period. It is a thin margin, but He wants to give us room to grow. However, there is a cost for this grace period. When God does something miraculous in that area of doubt, He *requires* us to change our thinking. We have no further reason to doubt. And He expects us to not only change our thinking, but to also change our actions.

In Matthew chapter 16, the disciples are in a boat with Jesus. They've just seen two incredible miracles recently: the feeding of 5,000 people from five loaves and two fishes, and again they saw a different group of 4,000 fed with only seven loaves and a few small fish. As they're in the boat, they realize that they have no bread for their journey and they're worrying about it.

> *When they went across the lake, the disciples forgot to take bread. "Be careful," Jesus said to them. "Be on your guard against the yeast of the Pharisees and Sadducees."*
>
> *They discussed this among themselves and said, "It is because we didn't bring any bread."*
>
> *Aware of their discussion, Jesus asked,* **"You of little faith, why are you talking among yourselves about having no bread?** *Do you still not understand?* **Don't you remember** *the five loaves for the five thousand, and how many basketfuls you gathered? Or the seven loaves for the four thousand, and how many basketfuls you gathered? How is it you don't understand that I was not talking to you about bread? But be on your guard against the yeast of the Pharisees and Sadducees." Then they understood that he was not telling them to guard against the yeast used in bread, but against the teaching of the Pharisees and Sadducees.*[5]

Jesus rebuked them for not changing their mindset about what should now be considered "normal" by them. They used to live in a world where having no bread was a problem. But then they met Jesus and they witnesses incredible miracles. Now, after seeing Jesus multiply food not just once but *twice*, He *required* them to change their mind about what was normal. Now, they no longer had any right to worry about what they would have to eat because they had seen Jesus address that problem with a miracle.

In the same way, we are required to change our mindsets when we see His miracles. No longer can we ever believe for anything less. Jesus did (and still does) miracles to show us what is *normal* in the kingdom of heaven. This revelation of heaven has a requirement: we must change our thinking. If a miracle happened once, we must always believe that it can continue happening. This is the lifestyle He was teaching His disciples and which we, as His continuing disciples, must also learn. Miracles demand a change of mind. When we have witnessed or heard about a miracle, we can never believe for anything less from that point forward. This is one of the ways the kingdom of heaven advances not only on earth, but also in the unrenewed parts of our mind.

Doubt may be allowed (but never excused) for a short time, but we must be very careful to be open-minded to the works of God. We must always give Him room to do the miraculous. There is a cost to see miracles in the form of our faith, but God will often give us a helping hand up to that next level. We must also be very careful not to let simple doubt become an entrenched unbelief that actively works against faith. Unbelief is a sin because it becomes an idol against God. Unbelief says, "I believe in my own reasoning, not in God's promise." God has given us the most powerful antidote to unbelief: faith. Every Christian believer has a measure of faith given to him or her by God. We must use our faith so we are good stewards with it, then we can ask God to give us more.

In Chapter 6, you will learn how to activate your faith. You'll learn the necessity of radical faith, why we must pay the price to pursue more of it, and how to increase in faith. You will then learn how to put your faith into action.

The Cost of Being a Kingdom Revivalist

John Wimber, the great preacher and revivalist, often used to say, "Faith is spelled R-I-S-K." He was absolutely right. Faith is more than a belief. It is a belief that must move us to action. If there is no action, then our faith is dead. James spoke about this in the book of James, chapter 2 when he said, "faith without works is dead."

But faith is believing in something that goes against our unrenewed mind's way of thinking. Faith goes against the natural, logical world. Faith is supernatural and operates in the spiritual realm. So how do we move past the fear that naturally confronts our faith? Like John Wimber said, we must take a risk.

When Peter stepped out of the boat to walk on the water with Jesus, he clearly knew it was a great risk. He had to have Jesus talk him into it! But he desperately wanted to be a walking sign and a wonder and he believed he could do it. He's the one who came up with the idea, not Jesus. When he stepped out, he took a huge risk. And it succeeded until his natural, unrenewed mind began to tell him how impossible it was.

I think the greatest enemy of faith isn't so much the enemy as it is our own minds. We so often talk ourselves out of risky adventures because we want to remain safe. But the apostles didn't play it safe. They took huge risks. Peter, who only weeks before had denied that he was even with Jesus during the crucifixion, decided to take a risk on the day of Pentecost and step out on the balcony of the upper room. He wanted to explain to the Jews below that a great event had just happened. He took a huge risk. This is how the apostles began a movement which spread the gospel around the world.

The interesting thing about risk, however, is that there is a possibility of failure. But in this case, I would prefer to call it a "lack of success." Yes, taking a risk may result in a lack of success. But it may also lead to a huge success!

We can't ever analyze a step of faith with the natural, unrenewed mind. The unrenewed mind doesn't understand the spiritual realm or faith. It will always come back with the same answer: Don't do it!

Miracles only come by faith. Faith requires risk. That means risk is a normal way of life for revivalists. Do you want to see miracles or would you rather play it safe?

As revivalists, our hope may be unfulfilled for a season. Perhaps we've been praying for someone's healing for quite a while and little to nothing seems to be happening. What does a revivalist do? Give up?

Revivalists understand one thing as a foundational truth: It is impossible to pray with expectancy and have nothing happen. God isn't standing there with his faith-meter saying, "Ohh... so close, but not quite enough! This prayer's a failure. Try again next time!" We don't know what's happening in the spiritual realm or what kind of demonic hindrances may be present. But we do know that God has given us power in our words, prayers, and faith. We know that He is so good, He wants the person to be healed more than we want them to. So we know that our prayers are effective.

We must press toward the mark, even if there doesn't *appear* to be any progress. Remember, we walk by faith, not by sight. We believe that something is happening in the spiritual realm and in their physical bodies. If we don't see any results immediately, that's okay. We'll keep going until it happens because we *expect* it to! This is why expectancy is so important, and why it is so much more powerful than hope. Expectancy demands an answer and won't leave until it gets one, while hope just sticks around until it gets bored, then it goes home. Hope should take us to expectancy because expectancy will get us to the miracle.

Another cost of being a revivalist is that we must always be adjusting our thinking when we hear or witness testimonies of God's power. Just as Jesus expected His disciples to change their thinking (renew their minds) after witnessing the multiplication of food, He expects us to do the same thing. Miracles are supposed to train us in the ways of the kingdom, they are to teach us what to expect, and they are to renew our minds. We can no longer hear testimonies as stories. Now, we are expected to become those testimonies!

And finally, we must have room in our theology for mystery. If we think that we have a full revelation of God or His kingdom, we are believing a lie. Not only that, but if we think we've fully figured out God, then our god is too small. I want to have some unexplained mysteries about God because that means He's bigger than I can comprehend! It also means I've identified some areas of revelation I can pursue. I can stir up a hunger in myself to ask God to reveal new parts of Himself and His love.

Isaiah 40:13 says, "Who has known the mind of the Lord?" Under the new covenant, we *can* know and have the mind of Christ. But are we fully there yet? Or will it take an eternity in heaven to ever fully know His mind? We must allow room for the growth process to occur.

Practically, this means that we need to be content with our questions about God, His kingdom, miracles, and supposed "failures" of faith. But being content doesn't mean doing nothing. We should actively pursue answers from God because He wants to reveal His mysteries to His children.

---

[1] *The Hayford Bible Handbook*, Jack W. Hayford, Thomas Nelson Publishers, p. 368, Truth-In-Action #3

[2] Mark 9:17-26

[3] Luke 8:43-48

[4] Ephesians 6:12

[5] Matthew 16:5-12

Chapter 6

ACTIVATION

Kevin Dedmon, long-time pastor and author of *The Ultimate Treasure Hunt*[1], summarized his pre-revival healing experiences by saying, "I used to have a 100% success rate when it came to healing the sick: I never prayed for anyone and nobody ever got healed." This describes my own pre-revival experience perfectly. But since I've started actively pursuing more of the gift of healing, I've gone up significantly from a 0% success rate.

Does that mean some don't get healed? Yes, too many. Does it drive me away from the gift of healing? Do I shy away from the sick, hoping I don't have to pray for them in case they're also not healed? Not a chance. Lack of success only drives me to God. I continually pray that God will increase his kingdom in me, that he would purify me, that he would help me mature and handle greater responsibility and power, and that he would teach me strategies for releasing his healing into the sick. I constantly ask God for more. God is honoring my prayers and He is giving me more.

I'm not afraid to fail. That was probably one of the most profound things I've had to learn. If I'm afraid to fail, I won't take risks. If I don't take risks, I'll do only what I know *I* can do. That means I'm likely to do things under my own human power. Which cuts out 100% of the supernatural power of God and His kingdom. By taking risks, I make mistakes and I don't always see the results I'm always expecting. But I do see miraculous things happening. And they're happening more and more as I press on toward the mark.

The Holy Spirit lives in me but He wants to live *through* me. I must live as a walking manifestation of His power. When people encounter me, they should encounter the God who lives *in* me, just as Jesus did. Many Christians want to live this kind of supernatural Christian lifestyle but they don't know how. They have faith but it is not activated in their lifestyle. If I believe that God can heal the sick through me, but it isn't happening (or not on a consistent basis), there needs to be an activation of that faith so that my belief will manifest in my actions. Activation is like the "start" button on an engine. The engine won't run unless it's started.

The gifts of the Spirit require a different shift in thinking. They require a new kingdom mindset that is in direct opposition to the natural, logical mind. But the only way we can activate the spiritual gifts is to adopt the godly, kingdom mindset of faith and put it into practice.

All of these spiritual gifts God has provided are available to any believer who is filled with the power of the Holy Spirit. All we have to do is pursue them. But there are some keys we can use to enable us to activate and walk in the gifts of the Spirit:

1. **Faith** *(page 93)*
2. **Action** *(page 103)*
3. **Risk** *(page 105)*
4. **Persistence** *(page 107)*
5. **Growth** *(page 109)*
6. **Practice** *(page 112)*

KEY #1: Faith

Faith is belief without evidence. Faith is choosing boldly and unswervingly to believe what God has said.[2] Faith requires a commitment so strong that nothing can shake it. Christians are called "believers" because we firmly believe all of God's promises and we seek the fulfillment of them.

James 2:14-26 says,

> *What good is it, my brothers, if a man **claims to have faith but has no deeds**? Can such faith save him? Suppose a brother or sister is without clothes and daily food. If one of you says to him, "Go, I wish you well; keep warm and well fed," but does nothing about his physical needs, what good is it? In the same way, **faith by itself, if it is not accompanied by action, is dead**.*
>
> *But someone will say, "You have faith; I have deeds." **Show me your faith without deeds, and I will show you my faith by what I do**.*
>
> *You believe that there is one God. Good! Even the demons believe that—and shudder.*
>
> *You foolish man, do you want evidence that faith without deeds is useless? Was not our ancestor Abraham considered righteous for what he did when he offered his son Isaac on the altar? You see that his faith and his actions were working together, and **his faith was made complete by what he did**. And the scripture was fulfilled that says, "Abraham believed God, and it was credited to him as righteousness," and he was called God's friend. You see that a person is justified by what he does and not by faith alone.*
>
> *In the same way, was not even Rahab the prostitute considered righteous for what she did when she gave lodging to the spies and sent them off in a different direction? As the body without the spirit is dead, so **faith without deeds is dead**.*

James talks about the futility of faith without action. Faith is more than a feeling, it is more than a core belief. Faith requires action! If I receive a letter from the IRS that says I can claim a $1,000 refund if I just visit their office, but I never go there to claim it, then all I have is a worthless letter. If I truly believe the letter and if I really want the $1,000, I must do something about it. **Faith *requires* action**.

Hebrews 11:6 says something we've all heard a hundred times. "Without faith, it is impossible to please God." But there's more to that powerful verse. "Without faith, it is impossible to please God, because anyone who comes to Him must believe that He exists and that He rewards those who earnestly seek Him."

Faith is like a power line. We need power to do anything supernatural. The power exists in God's heavenly realm. The way we access that power is through our faith. So we shoot our faith "power line" toward God until we reach His power, and then suddenly when it connects, our power line is energized which sends His power into and through us. But here's the interesting thing about power lines. They can be different sizes. Think of the thin black cord that runs from your cell phone to the black wall plug. This black cord is carrying a relatively small amount of power. Now imagine the thick power cables that run from hydroelectric dams to power substations. These are carrying incredibly huge amounts of power. If you try to run that much power through the thin little black cord that powers a cell phone, the black cord would instantly melt under that kind of power. It simply isn't capable of carrying that much power. The size of the power line determines the amount of power it can carry.

Our faith works much the same way. The amount of faith we have for a specific supernatural action often determines the amount of God's power available to accomplish it. God limits His power to the size of our faith. But remember, faith requires action. Maybe you conceptually believe that God can regrow an amputated hand right in front of you. But if you see somebody with an amputated hand, will you run up to them and put your faith into action? At that moment, you'll know how much faith you have. Small faith in action releases small power. Big faith in action releases big power. God has called us to radical faith so we can see radical power.

How Do We Increase Our Faith?

Faith is like a fire. It needs fuel. If you want to increase a fire, you increase the fuel source. One of the fastest ways to increase the fuel source for your "faith fire" is to get a hold of testimonies. First, read up on the miracles Jesus did in the Bible. Every miracle you read about is a testimony. The purpose of a testimony is to allow the hearer to be able to repeat it. So every testimony you read about or hear is being made available to you so you can repeat it. Not with words, but with action. Testimonies release supernatural grace and power to those who are hungry for it so that the testimony can be repeated. Many people hear testimonies as stories, totally missing out on the grace God is making available. But if you listen to or read a testimony with a hunger to make it your own, to be able to repeat it in other situations, you will take ownership of it and imagine yourself in that same situation. In this way, you are absorbing the grace God makes available and your faith will supernaturally increase.

Romans 10:17 says, "Consequently, faith comes from hearing the message, and the message is heard through the word of God." We can hear the word of God in testimonies that proclaim the glory of Jesus. By hearing testimonies of other things Jesus has done, our faith will increase greatly especially as we expect that testimony to be repeated in us or through us. If a testimony only entertains us but doesn't increase our faith, we're hearing it with our natural mind and not with our spirit.

A testimony should increase our faith and cause us to expect greater things to happen. Jesus rebuked his disciples when they were in the boat crossing the Sea of Galilee when they mistakenly thought

He was asking them to provide bread for lunch but they had almost none. He reminded them that they had just seen Him twice multiply bread and fish, so how could they still think the same way they used to? He expected them to change their minds about such worldly thoughts as "What if we don't have enough?" He rebuked them for not changing the way they think after having seen the power of the testimony. They continued to view the world through their natural, unrenewed mind instead of through their spiritual mind of faith.

Testimonies should not only increase your faith, they should also reveal to you another aspect of the "normal Christian life". Jesus now expects more of you since you have a new revelation of this normal way of life. Of course, it's not normal to the logical mind but we are commanded to "set your minds on things above, not on earthly things." (Col. 3:2)

We need to *expect* miracles, signs, wonders and healings to occur. God has promised it, so we are required to honestly believe it. Just as much as we honestly believe that we are going to live eternally in heaven with God when we die, we must also honestly believe that Jehovah Rapha, God Our Healer, has given us access to His healing power through the atonement of Jesus. Because we have access to that power, we can expect to receive it and to see its effects on people we are ministering to. Just meditating on the truths that "Jesus died not only to deliver us from our sins but also to bring healing for our physical bodies" and "Greater things will you do than I have done" for a few minutes is a great way to build up your faith. If God has promised something to us, we should believe it as absolutely as we believe in eternal life in heaven or in salvation through the death and resurrection of Jesus.

Consider the situation in Matthew 17:14-21. The disciples couldn't heal a boy with a demon that was manifesting with seizures.

> *Then the disciples came to Jesus in private and asked, "Why couldn't we drive it out?" He replied, "Because you have so little faith. I tell you the truth, if you have faith as small as a mustard*

seed, you can say to this mountain, 'Move from here to there' and it will move. Nothing will be impossible for you. But this kind does not go out except by prayer and fasting."

The disciples ask a simple question: "Why couldn't we drive out the demon?" Jesus responds, "Because you have so little faith. This kind of demon doesn't go out except by prayer and fasting." In other words, one way to increase your faith to higher levels is through prayer and fasting. Prayer is designed to bring you closer to God, to align your will and your spirit with His, and to be transformed by the supernatural renewing of your mind in ways that will increase your faith. Prayer is a way to encounter God in such a way that you leave a prayer session with greater faith than you started with, whether you were praying for a specific situation or because you simply wanted to be in His presence.

Fasting is a way to get your flesh to submit to your spirit. Your spirit says, "I will fast for a certain amount of days." Why? It makes no logical sense to deny your body something it needs and desires. The fact that it isn't logical is exactly why fasting is so important. It is an intentional way of training the flesh that the spirit is in control, and *not* the natural mind! Fasting does nothing for God. We're not proving our holiness or showing how much we want something. It is entirely for our own benefit. It is a powerful way for our spirit to be in control of our body, not our flesh. In this way, the faith of our spirit has more authority than the skepticism of our natural minds. Prayer builds our faith and fasting allows us to act on it in situations where our mind would otherwise be screaming, "That's not possible! Don't do that! It won't work!" This is what Jesus was referring to when He said His disciples had so little faith and taught them about prayer and fasting.

The power of God is only accessed through our faith. If we only believe God for "easy" things, we will only see that much power. But if we truly believe that God is the God of impossible things, that His power is so great it can cause amputated limbs to regrow in front of our eyes, that He can restore missing kidneys, and that He can restore neural pathways in a person's brain with Parkinson's disease, then we will have access to incredible power. Our faith releases God's power.

In his book *When Heaven Invades Earth*, Bill Johnson writes,

> "Part of our problem is this: we are accustomed only to doing things for God that are not impossible. If God doesn't show up and help us, we can still succeed. There must be an aspect of the Christian life that is impossible without divine intervention. That keeps us on the edge and puts us into contact with our true calling."[3]

FAITH IS COSTLY

Faith in action is very similar to a savings account. If you decide to start taking $100 a month and putting into a savings account, it's because you envision something down the road: a fat savings account. That's an awesome vision, but it's going to cost you something: $100 a month! Now you'll have less money to spend on other things and that could be a bit painful. It's going to cost you something to reach your goal.

Faith is just like that. When you step out in faith, it costs you because you honestly believe something but sometimes it doesn't seem to happen and your logical mind goes crazy trying to rationalize it in an understandable way. But it's at this point, when your mind is searching frantically for a solution (such as, "Maybe the gift of healing isn't for me" or "I guess God doesn't want to heal everyone"), that's where you have to stand on your faith. You have to stand on the promises of God that you believe in. The cost comes in telling your mind, "I don't care that I can't explain it, I still believe it anyway!" Okay, so you prayed for someone dying of cancer and they died. You had complete faith that they would be healed. That is a costly situation. But if you come out the other side with your faith intact, you've just deposited a huge amount of currency into your heavenly faith bank account. You have chosen to honor God with your faith instead of caving in to logic and reasoning that is firmly rooted in the natural realm. You have decided to live in the supernatural realm of heaven even though you don't have a satisfactory explanation. How can God not *love* that kind of faith? You have chosen to believe His promises. You've stood by Him, even when it was incredibly difficult. By honoring God with your faith in a difficult time, how could God not honor you? You have passed a trial and received greater favor and grace from God. When He searches the earth to find those with great faith that He can bestow greater blessing and power on, your name is going to be at the top of His list.

Faith is expensive. Great faith requires great actions and great risk. If something isn't incredibly risky, it probably requires very little faith. The reason something is risky is that there is, to the natural mind, a great chance that something won't work. The natural mind doesn't tend to believe in the supernatural because the supernatural exists on a different plane (the third heaven instead of the first heaven). So the natural mind sees any actions that result from decisions made in the third heaven (God's realm) to be incredibly risky. That is where faith is required. Faith is an action that is based on third heaven (supernatural) reality, not first heaven (earthly) reality. The natural mind will always have problems with this kind of action. That is why God requires faith, as a test to reveal what world we are *really* living in.

Faith pleases God. Without faith, it's impossible to please God. By putting your faith into action, you're pleasing Him. Honestly, He isn't concerned with the results. He sees your heart and the fact that you're willing to take a big risk for Him. If everything goes wrong and the results aren't what you hoped for, God is still greatly pleased because He sees your incredible level of faith. By continually stepping out in faith, regardless of the results, you are increasing in maturity and in favor with God. Even Jesus himself increased in favor with both men *and* with God! If Jesus could increase in favor with God, we certainly can. We do this by passing trials. A trial isn't necessarily a punishment or a negative thing. A trial is something that tests your faith. You can test your own faith! Just put it into action. By believing God's promises and acting on it, you've just passed a trial. Now you've shown a new level of maturity and faith which attracts the heart of God. He releases greater grace and anointing so that pretty soon, as you keep stepping out in faith, you're going to see greater results!

Faith doesn't care about negative results. It is unwavering. It knows that it knows that it knows that something will happen. Negative results are just minor potholes on the freeway to the hoped-for destination. They barely slow down the man or woman of faith. If you keep your eye on the destination and you know that you will get there, then nothing will get in your way. If you get distracted by the potholes or minor obstacles, pretty soon you'll slow to a crawl and you'll suddenly notice how bad the road is. Before you know it, you're more concerned with the dangerous road than with your destination. But if you're flying down the freeway at 120 miles per hour, the small bumps in the road and the little rocks scattered about are barely noticeable. Faith sees a destination and lets nothing stop it from reaching the goal.

A sanctified imagination is a great way to increase in faith. Evangelist Chris Overstreet used to spend almost every day in prayer, looking for ways to increase his faith for radical healings. During his prayer time, he would actually create space for his newly increased faith by practicing it. Literally! He would close his eyes and imagine a person with a broken leg in front of him. He would get out of his chair, kneel down, and look closely at the cast in front of him. He would place his hands on the imaginary cast and command it to be healed through the power of the Holy Spirit. He would release healing into the broken leg and call for restoration of the broken bones. Then he would pull back and see the imagined result: a young man walking on his now-healed leg. Chris would praise God for the miracle as if it really happened. He did (and still does) this kind of thing often to practice a lifestyle of supernatural ministry. This built up his faith because this became so normal to him that it was less scary.

A sanctified imagination is an imagination that is set apart for use by God so that He can reveal to us His dreams in our imagination and so that we can dream with Him. A sanctified imagination is like a set of training wheels on a bicycle. It allows us to practice difficult things until they become commonplace, so that it feels "normal," just as the miraculous lifestyle should be for Christians.

So, what do you want to do? What do you really want to do? Heal the sick? What kind of sickness? What kind of disease? What infirmities? What kind of cancer? Want to see someone's amputated arm grow back right in front of you? Okay, do it right now! Want to raise the dead? You can do it right now! This is the power of the sanctified imagination. You're creating a vacuum inside yourself by pushing your boundaries outward, creating room for God's power and anointing. God always fills our territory when we make room for Him. How can God refuse this kind of amazing invitation? He can't refuse because of His promises and He won't refuse because He wants you to do this more than you want to!

Chris Overstreet practiced healing the sick many times in his prayer sessions. Then, when he came across people who had the same need for miracles he'd already practiced, he had no fear. During these sessions, he made room for an increase of faith. God honored his hunger for the miraculous so that Chris was able to release healing into the people he ran across in his daily life. Now he is an awesome evangelist, able to offer people a supernatural encounter with the living God. Many people have been healed as a result of the faith increases he acquired during his "practice" sessions.

What do you envision in your sanctified imagination? What do you really want to see happen through you? If you can dream it, then with the power of the Holy Spirit you can do it!

FAITH MOVES HEAVEN

Jesus began his public ministry when he attended a wedding that had run out of wine. His mother knew who He was and had great faith in Him. Because of her faith, she put her faith into action and moved heaven.

Jesus wasn't yet "scheduled" to begin His ministry. In John 2:4, Jesus answers her request by saying, "It is not time for me to work yet." Not concerned with His reply, she immediately told the servants, "Do whatever He says." She knew without a doubt that Jesus could do this miracle and she wouldn't take no for an answer.

Mary's faith in Jesus put a demand on heaven, and heaven naturally responded. God is attracted to faith because it pleases Him greatly.

THESE SIGNS SHALL FOLLOW THOSE WHO BELIEVE

I titled my book *These Signs Shall Follow* based on the powerful message Jesus spoke to us in Mark 16:15-18:

> *"Go into all the world and preach the good news to all creation. Whoever believes and is baptized will be saved, but whoever does not believe will be condemned. And* **these signs will accompany those who believe***: In my name they will drive out demons; they will speak in new tongues; they will pick up snakes with their hands; and when they drink deadly poison, it will not hurt them at all; they will place their hands on sick people, and they will get well."*

Many Christians have read this passage and wondered why these signs don't seem to accompany us today. This has actually become a sickness in the church which has a name, Cessationism, referring to the theory that miracles and the gifts of the Spirit have ceased. The whole idea of Cessationism arose out of the theory that Jesus was only saying these signs would be around for a short time while the Bible was being confirmed as the Word of God. Jesus spoke these words to His disciples as a promise and He never rescinded that promise. Today, we are still His disciples. We are still commanded to "go into all the world and preach the good news," so we still have legal access to the rest of the promise.

So why don't these signs seem to accompany us? Probably because we haven't believed! Mark 16:17 says these signs will accompany those who *believe*. Yes, every Christian believes in salvation. But if we don't believe in healing, miracles, signs, or wonders, these signs won't be following us.

If we don't believe that sick people will be healed when we place our hands on them, then we probably won't place our hands on sick people. Or if we do, we may not be confident that they will be healed. Our own doubt or fear may get in the way of the healing. The only way these signs will accompany us is if we honestly *believe* they will.

Because faith requires action, we must also take action on what we believe. We must take this promise to the bank, knowing that every promise from God is for us, and we must expect Him to fulfill that promise. When we believe that "these signs shall follow," and we act on that belief, God will fulfill His promise.

KEY #2: Action

Faith without works is dead. If we believe something, we must act on it or our faith has no substance and is based on deception. If we truly believe something, we will act on it. If we don't act on it, it's because we don't truly believe it even though we think we do… thus, the dangerous deception.

Acting on faith is easy. In the words of a famous slogan, *just do it!* If you believe in the power of God and believe you have the gift of healing, then act on it. Next time you see somebody who is sick, ask them if you can pray and get them healed. Faith in action pleases

God *more* than faith without action because it is true faith. Remember, you're not praying for the sick because you want your success rate to increase. You're doing it because it is God's will and you want to be obedient to His will. You're doing it to please God! With this in mind, it really doesn't even matter what the results are. Simply doing it is enough to please God. He isn't concerned with your success rate because the second you put your faith into action, you have already succeeded! So don't worry about results. Don't slip into a performance mentality. If you see a sick person and feel an urge to pray for them and you suddenly remember that you've had more failures than successes, this is where you'll know if your motives are to perform for your own success or to please God with your faith and obedience. Forget the previous results and just do as Jesus did: go to every sick person and offer them a supernatural encounter with the living God. Forget results. Let God figure that out since it's His job to come through after you've put your faith into action.

When I received the gift of healing, suddenly I had to put my faith into action. I didn't feel any different than before I had the gift. So I had to understand by faith that I had received it. Regardless of the fact that I didn't feel any different, I had to act on what I believed I had received. I had to pray for the sick, knowing that I now possessed something I didn't have before. I started praying for the sick with a newfound faith. But still, I saw very little breakthrough. Sure, a few people got healed but many more didn't. This was frustrating at first until I realized I needed to ignore the "failures" and praise God for the fact that people *were* being healed! This was the first time in my life people were honestly being healed as a result of my faith declaration and prayer as I allowed the Holy Spirit to do His work through me. That was worthy of praise to God! I had to ignore the successes and failures and just keep going, trusting that God would honor my activated faith and bring the results in His own way. As long as I take action, my job is done. It's God's job to bring the healing or to do the miracle. It's only my job to make declarations, release His power, and take risks because of my faith.

KEY #3: Risk

Why do people believe in and want supernatural ministry, but they don't have it? Often, it's because they aren't willing to make any mistakes. They aren't willing to fail as they attempt risky things. Great success requires great risk. But great risk brings great mistakes. Successful people make many mistakes. But they learn from them which is why they become successful people. This applies to education, politics, business, research and development, and it certainly applies to the spiritual gifts and the Christian walk of faith.

Proverbs 14:4 says, "Where no oxen are, the manger is clean, But much increase comes by the strength of the ox." Oxen produce messes but they also produce increase. You can't have increase without problems. There is no such thing as a perfectly clean revival. The human body has a waste disposal system. The church body needs one. Even Jerusalem had a refuse gate[4].

What if we get a bad or wrong prophetic word as we're developing a prophetic culture? One word: FLUSH! Get over it. Have grace. Move on. God allows us to make mistakes as we're pursuing Him. We need to allow others to make honest mistakes as they're pursuing God's promises. Where there is a culture of grace, there is a culture of growth. If you're too afraid to make a mistake, you will not grow because you will not take risks!

Elbert Hubbard said it well: "The greatest mistake you can make in life is to be continually fearing you will make one."[5] And Theodore Roosevelt said, "He who makes no mistakes makes no progress."

Learn from your mistakes. Don't be afraid of them and don't let them hinder you. They are an important part of the learning process. Ask the Holy Spirit to help you learn from them in supernatural ways. Then your learning will go beyond what your natural mind can learn and understand.

God wants radical believers who live on the extreme edge. An old saying goes, "If you're not living on the edge, you're taking up too much space!" It is only by living on the edge, attempting absolutely impossible things, that we will thrust ourselves into the realm of miracles. If we attempt things that are safe, we will walk in our own confidence instead of having radical faith in God. Putting ourselves in a place of great risk means we must rely on God's promises and His goodness. We must believe that God is our greatest cheerleader and that our identity as Christians means we are called to expand God's kingdom by establishing it on earth. We are called to the miraculous lifestyle, and in so doing, we are called to bring great glory to the name of Jesus who gave us free access to the Holy Spirit. The Holy Spirit longs to glorify the name of Jesus. But He won't be glorified if the only thing Christians do is show up at church on Sunday morning, listen to a sermon, then go home. Enough of that! The Holy Spirit wants us to utilize His great power as we attempt the "impossible." When humanity sees the sons and daughters of God doing incredibly miraculous, supernatural things, they will see and know that God is a God of power and love. They will come running to God, wanting to know Him. They will want our lifestyle. The lifestyle of a Christian should be the envy of the world.

But the true Christian lifestyle requires great risk.

I'll never forget the first time I went up to somebody in a wheelchair in a retail store and asked if I could pray for her to be healed. I was with a friend (ministry is much easier two-by-two!) and we both went up to this woman, but I don't think I've ever been more scared in my life. We asked if we could pray for her to be healed because we knew that God wanted to heal her. She very politely declined our offer of prayer. I was both relieved and surprised. Relieved because I know my faith wasn't quite up there yet (this wasn't long after I had acquired the gift of healing and my faith was still in the radical growth process). And surprised because I thought, "Doesn't she realize God can heal?" Obviously, I had two mentalities warring in my head: my natural, logical mind which is naturally skeptical of supernatural things and my spirit man which believes anything is possible with the power of God.

We didn't see a healing that day, but we did see a huge success. We went up to somebody and offered the healing power of God, something I had *never* done while "out and about" on my daily business. I was incredibly scared because it was such a new experience and it was a huge risk for me to take. But we both did it! That was a phenomenal success, regardless of whether or not a healing took place. I know God honored our hearts and our faith. And I know He increased our faith and our anointing because we were good stewards with what we had. When we are good stewards, God gives us more. Risk is always worth it because it puts our faith into action, and that always pleases God.

I'm glad I was able to take this risk because it was only 8 months later that I was at a different retail store with several other people. We saw a woman in a wheelchair and went up to talk to her. She had polyneuropathy and we asked if we could pray for her. She let us do so and after more than 90 minutes of prayer, faith declarations, testing of the progress, teaching, prophecy and words of knowledge (all directed by the Holy Spirit as we pulled different spiritual tools out of our "toolbelt"), she was healed of five different physical problems. Best of all, she was able to stand and walk normally for the first time in ten years, where before she could only stand for 10 to 15 seconds at a time.

Great risk leads to great rewards.

KEY #4: Persistence

Persistence is the key to acquiring what we believe. Maybe you're attempting the miraculous but you haven't yet seen the breakthrough that you're hoping for. Do you give up? No, because you honestly believe God's promises are true for you and that leaves you no choice but to continue putting your faith into action! So you persist. Faith is the substance of things hoped for, the evidence of things not seen. Faith is the bridge between where you are (living a life without miracles) and where you expect to be (living a miraculous, revival lifestyle). Your faith is what carries you, but your persistence is what pushes you. Persistence doesn't give up because faith knows the value of God's promises. Faith knows that God must come through. Persistence says, "I won't stop until God's promise happens."

For a moment, consider persistence from God's perspective. What do you think pleases Him more? The man or woman who is so defiantly full of faith that nothing can shake his or her belief that God's promises are true? Or the person who says, "Well, I tried eight or nine times, honestly I did! And nothing happened. I guess God's promise isn't true. Or maybe it's just not true for me. Maybe God does play favorites with people and I'm nobody special." Obviously, you know God loves faith. You know how greatly it pleases Him. And that's what we, His sons and daughters, want to do most of all, right? We want to please our Heavenly Father because He is worthy and His promises are everlasting. As we keep our eyes focused on Him, He will come through on His promises. And then He will reward us greatly for our persistence.

Consider the parable of the persistent widow in Luke 18:1-8:

Then Jesus told his disciples a parable to show them that they should always pray and not give up. He said: "In a certain town there was a judge who neither feared God nor cared about men. And there was a widow in that town who kept coming to him with the plea, 'Grant me justice against my adversary.'

"For some time he refused. But finally he said to himself, 'Even though I don't fear God or care about men, yet because this widow keeps bothering me, I will see that she gets justice, so that she won't eventually wear me out with her coming!'"

And the Lord said, "Listen to what the unjust judge says. And will not God bring about justice for his chosen ones, who cry out to him day and night? Will he keep putting them off? I tell you, he will see that they get justice, and quickly. However, when the Son of Man comes, will he find faith on the earth?"

Our persistence pleases God because it shows faith in action. By continuing to pursue what we know is out there, we can't help but have a massive encounter with the power of the Holy Spirit. Every great revivalist in history got a vision for what they wanted as they read God's word. They put their faith into action and pursued that vision fervently, knowing they could have it if they just kept going after it. And every revivalist in history got what they envisioned. In fact, they got far more than they imagined.

What do you envision? Whatever it is, try multiplying it by a hundred or a thousand. God is infinite. We can't out-imagine Him.

KEY #5: Growth

In order to grow the spiritual gifts, we must practice them (see Key #6 below for more on Practice). Practice results in greater confidence, greater experience, and greater growth.

But we can also grow in power and anointing in many other ways:

- **Recognize that the Holy Spirit is given without measure**

    We are the ones who provide the measuring cup which is limited by our faith, holiness, and expectation. Increased faith and increased holiness lead to ever larger amounts of the Holy Spirit. God has not provided a maximum amount. God is infinite and wants to give us as much as we can handle. There is no ceiling or limitation. So we need to be constantly pushing our boundaries outward, making room for more of the Holy Spirit's power and anointing. Then we need to constantly ask the Holy Spirit to fill us.

- **Be desperate and hungry for more**

    We must be constantly asking for more. Cultivating hunger and faith in ourselves will help us to passionately pursue more of the Holy Spirit. Because there is no limit, it is up to us to constantly be seeking. God never turns away a hungry person who comes in faith, expecting to be satisfied. But it takes a mature person to not grow complacent or comfortable. Even as we are experiencing the "more" that we've been asking for, we must again cultivate new hunger and pursue it. There is always more waiting for us! God gives it to those who hunger for it.

- **Pursue purity**

    As we yield more of ourselves to God, He is able to clean away the selfishness, the sinfulness, and the wrong attitudes that can quench the power of the Holy Spirit. In chemistry, something is considered pure when it has no traces of any other substances in it. Water is considered pure if it has no impure or polluting elements in it. It is simply comprised of hydrogen and oxygen molecules bonded together, with no extra molecules of mercury, sodium, chlorine, or anything else. We must also be pure in our focus on God. As we continually yield ourselves to the will of God, He is able to remove the impurities in us. Soon, our will and God's will become one.

    What happens when your will becomes perfectly synchronized with God's will? This is what happens: You will be able to do whatever you want, and God will still do it... because your will has been conformed to the Father's will. He will be able to trust you with His power because He knows you only desire to bless others as He also wants to do. He knows you want to bring healing and restoration to people, just as He wants to do. He knows you cry out for justice as He does. He can trust you with His raw power because His will has become yours. So at that point, you will be able to do whatever you desire… and God will do it. That is the power of purity!

- **Impartations**

    Find others who have strong giftings such as people with incredibly accurate and specific words of knowledge or people with great healing anointings. Ask them to impart a greater anointing to you through spiritual impartation (to pass on a gift or an anointing through the laying on of hands as in Acts 8:17) and through giving (freely you have received; freely give). Ask if they will teach you some practical ways that they use their gift. You may learn some new techniques from them.

As we pursue growth in the use of the spiritual gifts, sometimes we may not see the results of our "pushing the boundaries of our territory outward." We may fight and push, constantly seeking after a particular breakthrough or a new level of anointing, but we ourselves may never see it. Does this mean we failed? No. We are not merely individuals, we are a church body. And we are not simply limited to the body of people alive at this moment. All through history, from the time Jesus left earth until the time He returns, all who believe in and follow after Him are His body. Our passionate pursuit for the next level in the kingdom of God will ensure that it is easier for others in the body, both now and in the future. Even if we don't live to see the specific breakthrough we're looking for, our children or their children may reach it. We are called to advance the baton along a running track, as in a relay race. Each runner's goal is to take it as far as the next person, knowing that only the final runner will get it across the finish line. But the victory belongs to every runner on the team because it requires passion and excellence from every team member. Don't ever assume that, just because you've passionately pursued something and haven't reached it yet, that your efforts of faith have been wasted. God never ignores faith. But He lives outside time. We need to consider things from a heavenly perspective, not an earthly one (Col. 3:2). All those forerunners who ran the race before us are now watching us, to see what we will do with the baton. Will we advance the kingdom? Will we be the ones who will finally push a particular baton across the finish line? Or will we consider that the finish line is impossible for us to reach so why bother even trying if we will never see the fruit of that labor? Which person do you think God is more pleased with?

KEY #6: Practice

If we're going to become good at anything, it's going to require practice. This applies to golf, words of knowledge, swimming, crochet, the gift of healing, stamp collecting, and prophecy. The more you do something that is difficult and challenging, the better you'll become at it. Experience only comes through practice. Practice is necessary because something is difficult at first. Golf is difficult because you need to train your body how to swing the golf club perfectly in order to get the ball where you want it to go. The first few times you swing a golf club, the ball will probably go anywhere but where you expect it to go! Do you give up and assume you're never going to be any good? No, because you understand the need to practice. And in fact, practicing golf is for many people an incredibly enjoyable activity. Likewise for me and many other people, practicing prophecy is incredibly enjoyable and it's very healthy for the body of Christ.

I've often asked people if I can practice the gift of prophecy with them by giving them a prophetic word. They know I'm only asking because I want to become more skilled at it, but I've never been turned down! They get something they want, and I get something I need: more practice. The more I practice prophecy, the more in tune with God's Spirit I become so I can get clearer words and pictures.

The more I practice the gift of healing, the more skilled I am at discerning the cause of sickness, disease, and pain in people's bodies. And the more I practice, the more I realize I don't know! So I go back to God and ask Him what I can do to become better. I understand my strengths and weaknesses and I ask Him to teach me how to become better at it. And sure enough, He has been answering me!

Practice is required because the gifts of the Spirit can be difficult at first, just like any challenging activity. But they are also incredibly rewarding because progress is so easy to make. There will be many moments of frustration, just like when you spend your first day at a golf driving range and you hope you can get the ball where you want it to go but instead it goes somewhere else. To prevent frustration, you need to have a passionate vision for yourself. In your imagination, you need to be able to see yourself living a miraculous lifestyle. Maybe you need to look at a healing revivalist and say to yourself, "Yes, I can become like him." Just like many people are inspired by Tiger Woods. They spend many hours practicing golf because they want to become like him, and because they know he himself spent many hours practicing as a child for many years. There are three reasons he has become so skilled at golf. Practice. Practice. Practice.

Paul instructed Timothy to "practice these things, devote yourself to them, so that all may see your progress." (I Timothy 4:15) The Message Bible phrases it even better as "cultivate these things, immerse yourself in them". By immersing ourselves in a culture of radical faith, seeking after more of the dunamis power available through the Holy Spirit expressed in our spiritual gifts, we will soon see the results for which we are hoping and expecting.

As we are practicing the spiritual gifts, we need to expect mistakes. But we also need to learn from them and to clean up our messes. Remember again that Proverbs 14:4 says, "Where no oxen are, the manger is clean, But much increase comes by the strength of the ox." You can have a clean manger but not much increase. If you want increase, expect some messes (mistakes). That's part of our learning process.

Let me offer a very direct challenge to you that will help to break any performance mentality you may have, because this challenge certainly helped me. If you don't make at least three mistakes in the next month, you're not trying hard enough. You shouldn't try to fail, but you should attempt things that are so difficult and impossible that you achieve some failures in your attempts. Learn from mistakes! You will only grow if you try things that are way beyond your comfort zone and your experience level. You will make mistakes and you may have some frustrating moments, but you'll also grow in ways you probably can't imagine.

In practicing the spiritual gifts, I've found it's incredibly beneficial to find other people with whom I can practice. So find some fellow passionate "students" of the gifts. Maybe create a home group where the theme is "practicing the spiritual gifts." There, you can create a safe environment for practice where everyone is required to try these things and there is no condemnation for mistakes. In such a healthy environment, every person will find themselves growing very quickly because they'll have no fear of trying these things and learning along the way. As a student is learning how they themselves hear prophetic words, they can try other methods just to see if that works for them or not. They won't have to worry about what the recipient might do with a strange word that may not be from God but from the person. Feedback can be given, not as criticism, but in the form of healthy ideas on how to become better. You can try giving a prophetic word to somebody in the home group, then ask them, "How did that word make you feel? Did you feel the heart of God in it? Was my delivery okay?" Feedback like this is crucial to building up your confidence in your ability. For more information on creating a safe environment for practicing the spiritual gifts, see Chapter 4 on "Culture."

How To Become Activated

Pastor Hedley Palmer has this to say about the importance of action as we seek to release the Holy Spirit's power (*dunamis* in the Greek):

ACTIVATION

> *Dunamis is the word from which we get our word dynamo. The dynamo was much used in motor cars, now we use alternators, but the same principle is applied. Movement produces power... whilst there is no movement, there is no power production.*
>
> *Mark is the Gospel of ACTION. Everything moves quickly in his book. The last verse is very revealing: "And they went forth, and preached everywhere, the Lord working with them, and confirming the Word with signs following."*
>
> **When they began to move, God moved.** *When they worked, God worked with them.*
>
> *We must learn more about the dunamis. Its first principle is that it is a latent power capable of reproducing itself. It is always there, and* **reveals itself immediately when there is action.** *So many people are waiting for God to move.*
>
> **When you move, God will move.** *The power will always be provided. You work in the will of God, God will work with you. Work by the Spirit, the Spirit will produce the dunamis.*[6]

It sounds blasphemous to suggest that we can move the Holy Spirit. It isn't blasphemy, it is faith in the identity and responsibility God gave us. We are co-laborers with Him. We are sons and daughters of the King. We are no longer servants, we are now friends. Because of this identity, we can move the Holy Spirit just as He is free to move us. It is a relationship, not a dictatorship. We are not slaves to His movements. He invites us to come up with our own ideas, to look for our own opportunities, to dream with God and then to use His power to make it happen. He is waiting for us to take action. He is waiting for us to GO so that He can work with us and confirm His word with signs following. This is how we activate the gifts of the Spirit.

Activation simply means "taking action to allow God to move through us." This requires us to move by faith, not by sight. We won't always feel confident to take a step of faith, but if we really believe in who we are (our identity) and in the responsibility God has placed upon us (Matthew 10:8), then we can take action which results in activation.

---

[1] Kevin wrote a great book about supernatural evangelism called *The Ultimate Treasure Hunt* available through Destiny Image Publishers. I highly recommend this book to learn more about how to work with the Holy Spirit using words of knowledge to find people in the community that God is highlighting to whom He wants to give a divine encounter that day.

[2] *The Hayford Bible Handbook*, Jack W. Hayford, Thomas Nelson Publishers, p. 352

[3] *When Heaven Invades Earth*, Bill Johnson, p. 110, Destiny Image Publishers

[4] Nehemiah 2:13

[5] http://www.quotationspage.com/quote/26991.html

[6] From sermon notes by Pastor Hedley Palmer
Original Web Page:
http://www.iclnet.org/pub/resources/text/hpalmer/snotes/serve-3.txt
Permanent Archive Page:
http://web.archive.org/web/20060211175745/http://www.iclnet.org/pub/resources/text/hpalmer/snotes/serve-3.txt

Chapter 7

AN INTRODUCTION *to the* GIFTS

The gifts of the Spirit are for everyone. Perhaps you've been taught that some gifts are only for some people, but I'm here to tell you by experience that all of the gifts are for every believer.

We are Jesus' disciples. We are to talk like him, look like him, love like him, walk like him, and do the same miracles he did. Whoever claims to live in him must walk as Jesus did (1 John 2:6). Who are we to be Jesus to? The world around us.

We all work with people who need a manifestation of Jesus in words and power. We go to the grocery store and interact with people whose hearts are crying out for a revelation of the Savior. Must these people really wait until a "minister" comes to them? No, *you* are the minister, so you are empowered by the Holy Spirit to manifest Jesus to them. After all, Jesus lives in you. Your hands are His hands! Your mouth speaks His words! You have the mind of Christ! Your renewed mind has the same thoughts that Jesus has! Jesus expects you to reveal Him to the world around you. At the grocery store, at work, on the bus, to your neighbors, and to your family. It's an awesome responsibility that we must all live up to.

In 1917, healing revivalist John G. Lake said,[1]

> *All that Jesus was to the world, He purposed that the Church of Christ should be. First, He blessed the world through His own physical personality. Second, He established a physical body composed of many members, joined in one by the Spirit of God.*
>
> *When He established the second body, the Church, He **never intended** that it should be of **lesser authority** or of **lesser power** than the first. It was His real purpose that the second body, the Church, should exercise and fully accomplish all that the first had done. [emphasis added]*

We can't stand before Jesus in heaven one day and have Him ask us, "Did you reveal Me to the world?" and respond, "No, I wasn't a pastor or a leader, I was just a church member." As a member of the Body of Christ, it is our job! For each person, that will look different because each is a different part of the body. But each person is required by Jesus to manifest His glory on earth and to establish His kingdom on earth as it already is in heaven.

Manifesting Jesus to the world is your identity and your privilege. Displaying the raw power of God on earth is your inheritance. You can choose not to do so because God honors your will. You can let fear keep you from living a miraculous life, but all of us will stand before Jesus one day. What will our answer be to the great question, "Did you reveal Me to the world? Did you glorify My name on earth through the power of my Holy Spirit?"

Maybe you're afraid to step out into the spiritual gifts because you don't want to screw anything up. Maybe you think that if you make mistakes, it's because you don't really have the gift or that God is judging you based on your performance, or that you may seriously wound somebody and you don't want to take that risk. Those are all very valid points… for anyone not a member of the Body of Christ! But you, being a member, have a very high calling. And even more, you have the greatest cheerleader in the universe: your Father God in heaven is watching you and cheering you on. He is like the perfect earthly father that never sees the honest, simple mistakes his child makes but instead sees the determination and the passion in his child. He loves to watch his child grow and develop, learning through trial and error. He loves to see his child determined to succeed, no matter what the results look like now. And when his child becomes frustrated or discouraged, he is right there to comfort and inspire his child because he believes in him or her.

This is how your Heavenly Father looks at you. All of your Christian life, you have believed in Him. But don't forget, your Father believes in you! Accept His challenge to manifest His glory, to work signs, wonders, and miracles, to walk boldly in faith instead of staying in the comfort zone of doubt and apathy. Living on the edge may not be easy, but you'll have a lot of great stories to tell! And not just the amazing testimonies, but the (sometimes funnier) stories of how you took a great risk and had nothing happen. Living a life of miracles has a cost: with success comes failure. This is because you're living in the "risk zone". But with great risk comes great reward.

It's important to point out that "failure," in the context of risk, isn't a bad thing. Thomas Edison was adamant about the necessity of failure in accomplishing a great vision. When his assistant asked him why he wasn't frustrated with the many failed attempts to create a light bulb filament that would last more than a few hours without burning out, he said, "I have not failed. I've just found 10,000 ways that won't work."

Failure is a necessary part of risk. If you're not failing, you're not risking anything! Be okay with it, give yourself permission to attempt challenging things and be ready to see a lack of success. But also have a vision. Know that you will have success as you keep trying.

Edison was absolutely sure he could discover the exact material that would produce a long-lasting filament which would finally allow the light bulb to be mass-produced. He envisioned cities and homes lit up with the artificial light and he longed to see his vision become reality. He kept his eyes on that goal and let nothing, not even 10,000 failures, stop him. He accomplished his vision and literally changed the world.

You can have the gifts of the Spirit. You can heal the sick. You will raise the dead. You are going to be able to walk up to a random person while you're shopping and reveal the thoughts of God to them through prophecy. And the good news is, it won't take 10,000 failed attempts to get there. It is surprisingly easy.

How to Acquire the Gifts of the Spirit

In Matthew 7:7-11, Jesus said, "Ask and it will be given to you; seek and you will find; knock and the door will be opened to you. For everyone who asks receives; he who seeks finds; and to him who knocks, the door will be opened. Which of you, if his son asks for bread, will give him a stone? Or if he asks for a fish, will give him a snake? If you, then, though you are evil, know how to give good gifts to your children, how much more will your Father in heaven give good gifts to those who ask him!"

We may confidently ask the Father for any gift knowing that "everyone who asks, receives." But sometimes, there needs to be an asking, a seeking, and a knocking. We must do so with faith that we will receive what we ask for, but we must continue asking, seeking and knocking until we receive it. That is faith in action.

Paul speaks often about the gifts of the Spirit and encourages the believers to eagerly pursue and use them. In I Cor. 14:39, he says, "Therefore, my brothers, be eager to prophesy, and do not forbid speaking in tongues." Here, he lists two gifts of the Spirit and encourages everyone to have them and to use them. Paul understood the incredible value of the gifts of the Spirit which is why he taught so often on how and why to use them, and gave very practical advice on how to use them effectively. As Paul was writing to the Corinthian church in I Cor. 1:7, he thanked God because "you are not lacking in any gift."

And in I Cor. 12:31, he said, "earnestly desire the greater gifts." He knew that the body of Christ was meant to walk in power, and that power came through the Holy Spirit. But the Holy Spirit expresses Himself in us through the gifts of the Spirit such as words of knowledge, the gift of faith, prophecy, healing, etc. So Paul asked the Corinthian church to eagerly pursue the gifts.

There are two ways we can acquire these gifts from the Holy Spirit:

1. **Through Impartation**

    An impartation means that somebody who has a gift of the Spirit can "impart" or give that gift to us through the laying on of hands as we receive it by faith. Jesus said to his disciples, "Freely you have received; freely give." In Acts 8:17, Peter and John placed their hands on some believers and they received the Holy Spirit. Whatever gifts of the Holy Spirit we have, including the baptism of the Holy Spirit, we can give it away to someone else through impartation. If somebody wants the gift of healing, I have the ability to impart it to them through the laying on of hands and a few words of faith. I have imparted the gift of words of knowledge to people. Often after I tell people stories about words of knowledge, I will ask if they also want that gift. When they say yes, I tell them that I will impart the gift into them. Sometimes they hold out their hands as a prophetic act of receiving but no particular body position is required... just an open and hungry heart. I will usually place a hand on their shoulder to establish a physical connection with them. This physical connection occurs in both the natural realm and in the spiritual realm. The physical act of placing my hand on their shoulder is a prophetic act that allows the Holy Spirit within me to release something through my hand into them. All of this occurs in the spiritual realm.

I then say something like, "Thank you, Holy Spirit, for the gift of words of knowledge that you have given me. All of this ability you have put within me I now freely give to this person. I also give them all of my breakthrough, all of my freedom, all of my testimonies, and all of the grace you have continued to give me as I have used it and practiced it." We can not only impart the gift, we can also impart the grace and authority we have received in using the gift. By imparting this, we can help the person to reach greater levels more quickly. This is one of the important ways that the church body can accelerate into the power giftings.

After imparting the gift and the anointing into them, I ask them to try it out immediately as an act of faith. I want them to really understand and know they have it. Otherwise, the enemy will come quickly and start whispering deceptions like "I don't feel any different so I didn't really get anything," or "I'm never going to be able to do this." So I have them try it out so they feel comfortable using it. And I encourage them to keep practicing it so that using the gift becomes almost routine. If someone only rides a bike once, falls down, and then never gets back on it, that's a terrible shame. I want to encourage them to continue practicing the gift until they become incredibly skilled at working with the Holy Spirit.

When I have the person try out the gift, I'll give them something simple. For the gift of words of knowledge, I'll immediately tell them, "Ask the Holy Spirit to reveal something about me that you would have no other way of knowing about me, such as one of my parent's names or some object in my house that you've never seen but I would know about." They may get the first two or three attempts wrong but invariably they start to get them right! Once the person realizes that they have received an impartation of the gift, then they are confident that they can continue to practice it without me being around. I try to find ways to build their confidence so that after I leave, they're excited to continue using it.

2. Directly From the Holy Spirit

We can also receive a gift of the Spirit directly from the Holy Spirit. This involves simply asking, seeking, and knocking until they get it. If you don't have anyone helping you, then you'll need to be passionate, full of faith, and practicing your faith. After asking, seeking, and knocking, you'll need to try it out to see if you have it. Pretty soon, you'll discover that you do have the gift you've been pursuing. But I've found that this method of receiving a gift can require more self-discipline and faith than receiving through impartation. By asking another person, you will have access to somebody who can not only give you the gift through the Holy Spirit, but he or she can also coach you and teach you. This makes it much easier to know what it is you're getting, how to use it, how to practice it, and in what ways it can be used. You'll have somebody available to ask questions and to hear amazing testimonies that will get you fired up.

If you can't find somebody, definitely go straight to the Holy Spirit and ask Him directly. He wants to give you His gifts more than you want to receive them! After receiving it, ask Him to teach you how to use it. It may take more effort on your part to go this route because you (most likely) won't hear an audible voice of teaching like if you went to a person who has the gift. But the Holy Spirit is our teacher, so you can confidently ask Him to help teach you how to use it. It just takes some time to learn how to listen for His answer. It could come through your imagination as pictures or movies. It could come as divine revelation as you suddenly get an idea to try. Or the teaching could come three days later through a teaching CD that somebody gives you in which you hear an amazing revelation that you can't wait to try.

KEYS TO REVIVAL: HUMILITY, HUNGER, FAITH

Asking for and acquiring the gifts of the Spirit requires three things: Humility, Hunger, and Faith.

You need humility as you look at yourself and realize you don't have everything you need to live as a revivalist who can live a miraculous, faith-filled life. You especially need humility to walk up to somebody who has a gift and ask them to impart it into you. If you find yourself having any hesitancy about this step, it is probably due to some amount of pride. Maybe you're a well-known leader in the church and you don't want to be seen going up to a housewife who has an amazing gift of prophecy so you can ask her to impart it into you. Pride will keep you from your destiny. Humility is required in the pursuit of God's presence, His will, and His power. So humble yourself, go up to that person, and ask them to impart the gift into you.

Hunger is required because only those who know what they don't have and want it badly enough will be hungry enough to do something about it. There are many Christians who have no desire for the spiritual gifts because, for whatever reason, they aren't hungry for it. God will only give His gifts to those who hunger for it.

In a very poor country, hunger drives people to desperation. They will do things that would shock those of us in richer countries. People will steal food. They will beg for it. They will eat things out of a garbage can. They will eat animal parts that would make our stomachs churn. People do this because they are so hungry, they will do whatever they can to be satisfied. I know this is a stark analogy, but it is true in the kingdom of heaven. God wants to know: how hungry are you? Many Christians simply aren't hungry. They don't realize they're starving because deception has blocked their minds from knowing the things they're missing. Ironically, they're content to live on moldy bread and dirty water because they don't realize God is offering a gourmet feast for those who are looking for it. Can you smell the aroma of God's gifts? Does it make your mouth water? Does it get you to stand up and start looking around, trying to find the source of that incredible aroma? That is why God tempts us with the miraculous. That's why He gives us so many testimonies of miracles in the Bible. They're the aroma of heaven. Will we become so hungry for that lifestyle that we'll do anything to get it?

God hasn't hidden these things *from* us... He's hidden them *for* us. Proverbs 25:2 says, "It is the glory of God to conceal a matter; to search out a matter is the glory of kings." God has hidden things in order to separate those who don't hunger for these things from the rest of us who do. But He is like a father who hides Easter eggs for his children. He is going to make it easy for his children to find so that the hunt is fun and not frustrating. He isn't going to go in the backyard, dig a three-foot deep hole, bury the Easter egg, then cover it up with dirt while giggling madly as he thinks about how his kids will never find it. God hides things as a test to see how hungry we are. He values His gifts highly and He only wants to give them to those who desperately want them and passionately believe they can have them. When we have to jump over a hurdle to acquire something, we tend to value it much more highly. Though there may be a hurdle, His gifts are always free. We're not earning them. We're simply pursuing them, knowing they're ours to have.

We must pursue and acquire the gifts of the Spirit by putting our faith into action. Do you believe you've received the gift? Then use it! Try it out. This is putting your faith into action. You probably won't feel any different. Your hands probably won't glow. More than likely, you're not going to start levitating six inches off the ground. So what do you do? You believe Jesus' promise when He says, "how much more will your Father in heaven give good gifts to those who ask him." You believe you've received it. So try it out and see what happened! Faith always requires an action.

Gifts of the Spirit mentioned in the New Testament

God has given us access to many gifts. This is just a short list of the gifts that were mentioned in the New Testament.

1. Apostleship
2. Prophecy
3. Evangelism
4. Pastoring
5. Teaching
6. Healing
7. Miracles
8. Tongues
9. Interpretation
10. Wisdom
11. Knowledge
12. Faith
13. Discernment
14. Serving
15. Exhortation
16. Giving
17. Leadership
18. Compassion
19. Helps
20. Administration

Other Gifts of the Spirit

I believe there are more than the 20 gifts of the Spirit mentioned in the New Testament. The reason only 20 are mentioned is because these are the specific ones that Paul chose to teach on, but the principles that he gave us can apply to other supernatural gifts given to us by the Holy Spirit.

What other gifts are there? I believe there is a gift of evangelism. I believe this gift can be imparted by evangelists. I believe there is a supernatural gift of creativity and ideas. This gift is latent in every Christian believer, ready to be accessed through the power of a sanctified imagination that knows how to dream with God. The gift of craftsmanship, along with gifts of wisdom, understanding and knowledge, was given to Bezalel in Exodus chapter 31 so that he could make artistic designs for the house of God. I believe the gift of craftsmanship and other gifts relating to creative heavenly ideas are useful in a Christian's marketplace ministry. When all of the most inventive and useful ideas for a business are coming from Spirit-filled employees, God is going to get a lot of glory for it.

The gifts move and flow freely in a believer in such a way that you sometimes can't tell if it's a word of knowledge or a word of wisdom. Often, I've accidentally given words of knowledge when I think I'm giving a prophetic word. And often, I give prophetic words when I'm looking for words of knowledge. It's all from the same Holy Spirit. We don't need to put His gifts into individual compartments because the Holy Spirit moves freely outside of our boxes. Likewise, the combinations of the gifts can lead to what appears to be totally unique giftings. And mix into that our own unique histories, our unique ways of thinking, and our unique God-given abilities and you can see how the exact same gifts in two different people can manifest in completely different and beautiful ways.

I was on the prayer team at a prophetic conference at our church. After one of the evening sessions, those who wanted prophecy or healing were invited to come forward for prayer. The first woman I prayed for said she'd had back pain consistently for seven years. I prayed for maybe 30 seconds, declaring the kingdom of God in her body and commanding the pain to leave. I didn't ask God to do it. I used the gift of healing He has put within me to release the healing into her body.

After 30 seconds, I asked her how she felt. She said it was about 90% gone but there was still a little pain remaining. I told her God had healed her in that 90% and I thanked God for it, but I told her I would pray again because I knew we could get it to 100%. So again I released healing into her. Then I asked her how it was. She checked out her back, flexing and bending it a bit. She said she was now completely healed! The back pain was gone.

The next person who came up to me for prayer was a woman who'd flown all the way from New Zealand to attend the conference. She said she had both neck and back pain. I told her that not two minutes prior, I had just seen a woman get healed of back pain. She was excited so I began praying. After about 30 or 40 seconds, I asked her how she felt. She said she definitely felt the tangible presence of God on her and she said, "I'm claiming this healing by faith." As she said this, she was turning to head back to her seat but I stopped her and said, "Wait! Instead of claiming this healing, how about if I just get it for you? I'm in no hurry and I know God wants to see you healed right now." So she immediately accepted and let me continue praying and releasing God's kingdom.

As I started praying, I asked the Holy Spirit what to do. I didn't want to follow a formula, I wanted to follow the leading of God. I found myself again asking this woman how she felt. She said, "I feel the presence of God very strongly on me since you prayed for me the first time." Then she stared off into space for a second as she considered something. She turned back to me and said, "That's funny... I feel something attached to my neck." That was interesting! I asked her if she knew what it was. She furrowed her brow for a moment, then said, "No, but I don't think it's good." I said I'd ask the Holy Spirit to show me what it was.

I closed my eyes for a moment and pictured the woman. I pictured her neck and noticed something clearly sticking out of it: a large dagger was embedded into her neck all the way to the hilt, with a handle that was about 10 inches long. I zoomed in on the image and noticed a word written on the handle in large letters: ENVY.

I opened my eyes and said, "I see a dagger embedded in your neck and the word ENVY written on it. But I don't feel like it's from you, I feel it's from someone else who envied you in some way and either intentionally or subconsciously hurt you through hatred, anger, or bitterness."

She seemed amazed by the revelation. I said, "Here, let me pull it out." I got behind her, waited a few seconds as I pictured where it was on her neck, then I grasped this invisible dagger by the hilt and pulled it out of her neck. I tossed it onto the ground. The instant I pulled it out of her neck, she sank down to the ground as she started laughing joyously.

She stood back up quickly, saying, "I can't believe it, I actually felt it leave! I felt it come out of my neck. I could feel you pulling it out and now it's gone. That's amazing!" She was moving her neck around, checking it out. She was healed. She was praising God as she headed back to her seat.

One of the associate pastors was on the stage watching the 40 or 50 people being prayed for. As healings occurred, the prayer team ran up to him and reported each healing so he could say it into the microphone which built up people's faith. I went up and told him about the two women who'd just been healed and he called it out.

A few moments later, a man rushed up to me and said excitedly, "I have neck and back pain! Pray for me next!" He had just heard the testimony and he was ready to be healed.

I started to pray for his back but immediately felt the Holy Spirit leading me into the gift of prophecy. I started to get some strong prophetic revelation so I went with it. If the Holy Spirit is leading me in a specific direction, I'd rather follow His lead than operate on my own. So I started telling him the prophetic revelations I was getting for him.

After about 10 minutes of this, I felt the Holy Spirit lead me to stand behind him. I went around behind him while still keeping a hand on him, but I moved my hand to his back. As I stood there looking at his back, I could see something in my spirit. I saw a zipper on his spine. I stared at it for a second, sort of amazed and a bit unsure what it meant. I didn't see it with my eyes, I saw it in my imagination but it was put into my imagination by the Holy Spirit. So I stared at the zipper and said to him, "I see a zipper on your spine." Then I did what anyone would do with a spiritual zipper. I reached up to the back of his neck, grabbed the zipper, and unzipped it all the way down. I could now, in my spirit, see that the inside of his back was exposed. I could "see" (in my imagination) his muscles and spine that were exposed. I felt the Holy Spirit tell me to put my hand on his back. I did so, putting my hand right over his spine. I could immediately sense that my hand wasn't just on his back, it was inside his back. Knowing this, I asked the Holy Spirit, "What are you doing in his back?"

The Holy Spirit replied, "I'm replacing his spine of bone with a spine of iron." I asked the next logical question. "Why?"

He said, "I've given him more of my weighty glory, power and presence. His capacity to carry it needed to be expanded so he could contain it. It was so powerful on him, it was bowing him down and he needed a stronger 'spine' to carry the weight of it. I am upgrading his capacity to carry it." I asked if this had anything to do with his back pain. "Yes, his body misinterpreted his spiritual situation. His spirit knew there was too much weight on it, and his body misinterpreted it by manifesting pain in his back."

I then told the man what I'd just heard and seen. After I relayed it, he was visibly excited and ready to burst. When I finished, he clapped me on the back and said, "Wow, man, you are firing on all cylinders! I can't believe you just said all that! Let me tell you what just happened."

"Two weeks ago, someone gave me a prophecy. He said that he saw a zipper on my spine, and that God would replace my spine of bone with a spine of iron. You just repeated that exactly word-for-word! But after that first prophecy, I was asking God why he would do that. Why did I need a spine of iron? He didn't give me the interpretation. But today, He answered it through you!"

All three healings, one after the other, had similar pain symptoms. But all three required completely different actions to release the healing. Don't assume that all people will get healed through the prayer of faith. Sometimes it may require a prophetic act. Other times, God may want to speak His truth to them through your gift of prophecy. In speaking truth, God can release grace to break mindsets that have given sickness or disease a place of refuge in their body.

We shouldn't limit the gifts of God or the ways that they work together. Putting them in a box, not listening to the leading of the Holy Spirit, or simply trying to follow a formula is the quickest way to lose the anointing that releases miracles.

INCREASING OUR ANOINTING FOR SIGNS, MIRACLES, AND WONDERS

The kingdom of God is manifested through us in signs, wonders and miracles. However much (or little) anointing we start with, we need to be good stewards with it. Being a good steward with anything God gives us will result in an increase. Stewarding the anointing for miracles will cause an increase in that anointing.

So how do we steward the anointing? First, we use it. We can't compare ourselves to others around us and say, "I have so little anointing for this, why do I even bother? All I ever see is headaches being healed but Joe over there has an anointing for life-threatening diseases that are being healed!" Whether we have one talent or ten, God still expects us to use it and to increase it. So you have an anointing for the healing of headaches. Rejoice! There are people who are desperately waiting to be healed of painful and debilitating headaches. That healing will be as important to them as someone healed of a life-threatening disease.

As you steward what God has given you by using it at every opportunity, you will attract heaven's anointing for greater power and greater miracles. But it also helps to be hungry for more. Be actively seeking greater anointing and power. Ask God for it. Look for it. Read books about it. Listen to teachers who preach about it. Ask people for impartations for more. God always responds to hunger.

He wants to know... do you really want it? How much? Are you willing to step beyond your comfort level and your pride to get more?

Desperation for more is what unlocks rooms and storehouses in heaven that nothing else will unlock. Desperate people don't care what anybody else thinks of them. They will do anything they can to get more. This isn't about greed. It's about knowing our identity. And it's about knowing that the Holy Spirit is given "without limit," as it says in John 3:34. What, then, is the limit? Our hunger. Our expectancy. Our comfort level. Are we comfortable with the amount of anointing for signs and wonders that we have? Or are we going to boldly approach our Father's throne and ask Him for more?

God hides things for us, not from us. Desperate, hungry people seek and continue seeking until they find what they know is there by faith.

And finally, a simple but powerful way to increase in anointing is to find somebody who has more than you. Ask them to impart their anointing into you. Then believe you have received it. Take action on that belief by finding someone to release healing into. See what happens. After receiving an impartation, put a demand on heaven by trying it out. But do so with expectancy. Expect greater things to happen than before! This is how you grow in faith and anointing. You'll soon find yourself operating at amazing new levels of authority and power.

---

[1] *John G. Lake: His Life, His Sermons, His Boldness of Faith*, Kenneth Copeland Publications, p. 384

Chapter 8

PROPHECY

1 Cor. 14:39 Therefore, my brothers, be eager to prophesy.

A woman sat in a chair surrounded by a dozen or so other people. They were prophesying over her one at a time as the Holy Spirit revealed things to them. One man asked the Holy Spirit for a prophetic word for her. But all he could see when he looked at her was a yellow shirt. It seemed to be superimposed over her as if she was wearing it, but she wasn't actually wearing a yellow shirt. He was sure it was imagination.

He decided to ask the Holy Spirit what it meant. He got no response. He didn't know if he should even give it since it wasn't profound. It wasn't revelatory. It wasn't even that interesting! He was about to discard it, again thinking it was just his imagination, when the Holy Spirit gently prompted him, "Tell her."

He said to the Holy Spirit, "But I don't know what it means!"

The Holy Spirit again said, "Tell her."

So he said out loud, "I see you wearing a yellow shirt." He was about to start giving his own interpretation of what it meant. He figured he would talk about "the glory of God" or something, anything, so that it had more meaning.

But even before he could continue, she had already fallen off her chair onto the floor. She was laughing, crying, shouting, and thanking God at the top of her lungs. Everyone was startled and curious. This poor man was wondering what in the world he'd just said. It wasn't a profound word! Why was she reacting so powerfully to the "yellow shirt?"

When she pulled herself up off the floor and got back in her chair, she looked at him and said, "I know you don't realize what you just said. Let me tell you."

"My son has autism. I've been praying for his healing for years. This morning, I was feeling a little frustrated and I asked God if my son was going to be healed. If so, I asked Him to have somebody tell me they saw me wearing a yellow shirt. Obviously, I'm not wearing one. The only way you could've said that is if the Holy Spirit revealed it to you. That is my confirmation from God that my son will be healed! Thank you for giving me that prophetic word."

The gift of prophecy is an amazing gift that builds up the body of Christ by giving us specific words from God. When we hear God's personal voice for us, in the exact situation or stage of life that we're at, we can be reminded that God is concerned about the details of our life and that He wants to encourage us. Through the gift of prophecy, we get to learn God's "plans to prosper us, and not to harm us. Plans to give us hope and a future," as He says in Jeremiah 29:11. The woman with the autistic son got an encouraging word from God: "Keep pursuing your son's healing because I *am* going to do it!"

What Is the Gift of Prophecy?

The gift of prophecy allows the saints to build each other up through edification, exhortation, and comfort through the prophetic words of God. In 1 Cor. 14:3, Paul teaches, "But he who prophesies speaks **edification** and **exhortation** and **comfort** to men." Paul also considered the gift of prophecy to be the most important of the gifts of the Spirit specifically because it builds up the body of Christ. Instead of using our tongues to tear each other down, we can use the gift of prophecy through our tongues to encourage, love, and honor each other. God gives us access to His thoughts so that we can speak them out over people. How amazing is it to hear the thoughts of God spoken over you by another person? It's a beautiful thing. And the most amazing thing of all is the result. The person hearing God's voice is encouraged, built up, comforted, and knows that God sees them in a kind and loving way.

Even better, the person prophesying over the person gets to hear how God views that person. If you are prophesying over someone that you've never gotten to know, and suddenly you find yourself giving a prophetic word that is beautiful and heartwarming, you're naturally going to feel connected to that person from that point forward.

Imagine if you walked in on a conversation between a husband and wife, and you heard the husband telling his wife how much he adores her and why he is so smitten with her. You may not have known the couple before, but from then on you will always know the beautiful intimate feelings they have for each other. You will see the husband as a kind, gentle, and loving man who respects and cares for his wife. And you will always see the wife through the words that you heard spoken over her. Every time she does something that confirms those words, it will only reinforce what you heard. You will feel naturally drawn to them because intimacy is the product of a safe environment. The same thing happens with the gift of prophecy. Not only does it build up the recipients, it also unifies the body of Christ in a truly supernatural and powerful way. As God reveals His intimate heart for His loved ones through us, He causes us to see each other through God's eyes instead of our own. This is why Paul valued the gift of prophecy so much. And this is why a prophetic culture is so important. A prophetic culture creates an atmosphere of love, honor, and edification that unifies the body together.

EDIFICATION, EXHORTATION, AND COMFORT

Prophecy is for edification (building people up), exhortation (calling/drawing people to God), and comfort (God knows you and loves you in a personal way).

We don't prophesy negative things. Why not? People are already aware of their own sins. They know this through their own knowledge, the conviction of the Holy Spirit, or from the accuser of the brethren. They don't need prophetic people revealing negative things that are obvious to them because it's non-productive and doesn't produce hope. Most people already have a hard enough time looking at themselves in a positive, healthy way. God wants us to see ourselves the same way *He* sees us. That's why He speaks to us through the gift of prophecy: so that we know how much He loves us, cares for us, and so we know what amazing people He has made us to be! When we believe lies and deceptions about ourselves, we dishonor our Creator. God uses the gift of prophecy to build us up, stir us up, and cheer us up.

We are not like Old Testament prophets. Many times, their purpose was to bring correction to God's people, to restore them to God's plan and purpose. We who have the gift of prophecy are called to build up the body of Christ (edification), to exhort and bring people closer to God, and to bring comfort.

The Holy Spirit is referred to as the Comforter in the New Testament. One of the most powerful ways we can experience the comforting of the Holy Spirit is by receiving a positive, uplifting prophetic word from someone with the gift of prophecy.

Prophecy involves calling out the gold in people. Everyone already knows their own dirt. But when someone with the gift of prophecy sees inside them and calls out gold that the recipient didn't even know was there, what an incredible treasure that is! It builds up the recipient, it reminds them that God still loves them, and it brings great comfort. This is an especially amazing tool to use in supernatural evangelism. You never even have to use the word "prophecy." Simply by asking the Holy Spirit to reveal the gold in people, you'll be able to speak to them supernaturally, revealing things in people that may be so personal and beautiful, it can bring them to tears. When they realize that God has shown you some part of themselves that is good and beautiful, something they may not have known they had, they will become hungry to know the God of life, love, and kindness.

The gift of prophecy also brings divine revelation which is used in the edification, exhortation and comfort of believers. Prophecy reveals God's heart to man, it reveals His emotions, His longing, His calling to His people. But prophecy does so in a very personal way. Prophecy often speaks the *rhema* word of God in a specific season for a specific purpose. Every believer is in a different season, at a different level, and has different needs. The gift of prophecy allows each individual to hear from God about their specific needs and situations, whether as an answer to prayer or as a foretelling revelation of the immediate or long-term future.

PROPHESYING RESPONSIBLY

Imagine that you're still pretty new at the gift of prophecy. You're excitedly prophesying over anyone and anything that moves. At church, you come across a new Christian and ask if you can give them a prophetic word. They agree. You see a brief image of Africa and you excitedly tell them that they're going to Africa.

Okay, you're thinking you're hot stuff because you just gave an amazing directional word just like an experienced prophet and now Africa will have a new missionary on its way.

But meanwhile, this new Christian goes home in great confusion. "Africa? Africa?? I don't want to go to Africa. I think I'd hate being there!" But, being a new Christian and not wanting to displease God, they move there. And they hate it. But they believe it's God's will and they have no choice. After all, God spoke it through someone with the gift of prophecy, so it has to be the word of God, right?

Did God really speak it? And if He spoke it, did He really want you to reveal it?

The interesting thing about the gift of prophecy is that it can reveal the future. Just as an axe can be used as either a tool or a weapon, the gift of prophesy requires responsibility. Using it wrongly can hurt others, even though you don't mean to.

In this hypothetical case, let's assume that the person giving the prophetic word really did see an image of Africa. Just because you see something doesn't mean you're *required* to give it. The gift of prophecy comes through the opening of your spiritual eyes so that you can see and sense things in the spiritual realm. There are an incredible variety of things happening in the spiritual realm… it's not just limited to angels and demons. The gift of prophecy allows us to see what's happening. Just because we see it doesn't mean we're required to give it. When God opens our eyes, we're able to see anything that's there: good, bad, and ugly. God only wants us to reveal the good things. And He wants us to reveal it responsibly.

In this case, let's assume there really was a call to Africa on the person. But they're still a new Christian and they still need to grow close to God, they need to discover and learn their own gifts of the Spirit, they need to grow in the Word. They are nowhere near ready to go to Africa. God has placed a secret seed of this desire in their heart (which is what the prophetic person saw with his spiritual eyes) and that seed may take years to grow. One day, this man is going to realize how desperate he is to go to Africa. The day will come when he is going to plead with God to send him there, perhaps not realizing it was God who placed that desire in him in the first place! But just because you see something doesn't mean it's time to reveal it. This is why it helps to have rules and boundaries to keep you and the other person safe. By staying inside these boundaries, you can prophesy freely without leaving any huge messes behind.

As you are learning and practicing the gift or prophecy, there are four very important rules to follow so you don't cause problems. By following these rules, you will be in a "safe zone" in which you can move freely, knowing you'll protect and honor people properly.

1. **Do** try the word out on yourself first before giving it.

2. **Don't** give directional words, even if you see it clearly! Many churches (wisely) require that somebody be on a prophetic ministry team for a number of years before they are allowed to give such words. It takes time to grow into the prophetic gift and you don't want to leave a mess behind as you're learning to hear the voice of God and use wisdom in speaking it.

3. **Don't** prophesy mates (husband/wife), dates (new job on Thursday), or babies (two boys and a girl).

4. **Don't** give correctional or negative words.

In general, the easiest way to test a word you're about to give to ensure it will be properly received by someone is to try it out on yourself first. If you would appreciate hearing the word, then you know it's safe to give.

GETTING AND GIVING A PROPHETIC WORD

Prophecy is really easy. The reason most people have a hard time doing it is because they lack confidence. First, I'll show you how to get a prophetic word. Then I'll tell you how to build confidence so you won't second-guess everything you're getting which may prevent you from speaking it out.

First, you need to realize that God is always speaking. He is like a radio station transmitting antenna from which many different radio stations are sending their signals. At every moment of the day or night, there are always multiple signals being transmitted. Right now, as you're sitting and reading this page, those signals are flowing through the room. They're flowing through your body. You can't see them or sense them. The only way to turn those invisible but very real signals into something you can hear is by using a radio receiver. It converts the invisible radio signals into audible sound.

The gift of prophecy works exactly the same way as the radio receiver: it allows you to "tune in" to the airwaves as God is broadcasting multiple messages to everyone around you.

Because God is infinite, He is often speaking many different things *to each person* at the same time. As I participated in the prophecy class where I practiced the gift of prophecy, we would ask one person to volunteer to be prophesied over, then all of us would give prophetic words as we received them. I wondered how we could all be right. Shouldn't we all get exactly the same word? Then God revealed to me that He is saying more than one thing to them! Then a few weeks after that revelation, we were doing this same exercise in class. As the volunteer was sitting down in a chair in the middle of our circle of chairs, at that very moment he was sitting down I saw a brief flash of a prophetic vision. I saw a shining suit of armor on him, exactly like a knight would wear. As others began prophesying to him, one woman sitting on the other side of the circle said to him, "Just as you were sitting down, I saw you wearing a suit of knight's armor." I was absolutely shocked! I'd seen *exactly* the same thing! This was one of those times where she and I happened to tune into the same "radio channel" and we picked up the same message that God was speaking to Him. The more you practice in group settings, the more common you'll find this to be. It's also a great confirmation that you really are picking up God's prophetic messages when somebody else confirms your word, or you confirm theirs in this way.

Prophecy

Understanding that God is always speaking, it becomes easier to get a prophetic word. You don't need to ask God to make one up. You don't even need to ask Him to tell it to you. You just need to listen with your Spirit to what *He is already saying at that moment* for someone. God wants to have a personal, intimate relationship with all of His children, whether they know Him or not. He is always speaking to us, not out of condemnation or judgment, but as a friend speaks to another friend. For those who can't yet hear God's voice, you (with the gift of prophecy) have the ability to listen in on what God is trying to say to them. Then, *you* can be the voice! You can be like a telephone that allows them to hear the incoming call that God is trying to make. This is an amazing privilege that we have: to be God's voice to a generation that desperately wants to hear Him! As you reveal God's voice to people, you allow them to draw closer to His presence. Soon, they can hear God's voice for themselves. And they can hear God's voice for others. The gift of prophecy helps people draw closer to God. And it even helps draw people closer together to *each other*, as I talked about in Chapter 4.

God is always speaking, but obviously His first language is not English. Most of the time, you won't hear an audible voice of the Lord (in your ears or in your head). Generally, you will get the prophetic message through any of several different ways.

Different Voices of the Spirit

You can get a prophetic word in many different ways. It could be different every time you prophesy, or perhaps you will hear from God mostly in one way. Or, God may periodically change the way He speaks to you so that you learn to hear His voice in new ways.

These are some of the ways in which you can hear God's voice for a prophetic word. Please note this is not an exhaustive list.

- Imagination
- Memory / Recollection
- Bible
- Dream
- Vision
- Colors
- Numbers
- Feelings / Impressions
- Audible Voice
- Angelic Visitation
- Sound
- Smell / Aroma
- Physical Feelings or Sensations

Time to Practice!

Ready to try this out? Good. You can do this with nobody around or you can go find someone and ask if you can practice getting a prophetic word for them. If nobody is around, pick somebody you know so that your prophecy will have a "target."

Now, close your eyes. Ask the Holy Spirit to show you something about them through the gift of prophecy. Now remember to relax… I can feel you tensing up! You don't need to *try* to do this. The prophetic word comes from the Holy Spirit, not you. So relax and let Him speak to you. Give him a moment to reveal something in your imagination, since that is the most common way to hear His voice.

With your eyes still closed, watch what happens in your imagination. Did you just have a random thought pass through your mind? Check it out! What was it? Or did you see a very brief image in your imagination? Perhaps a blue car. Or a waterfall. Yes, it feels exactly like you made it up and you were about to push it aside so you could get a "real" prophetic word. Don't push it aside! That *is* the prophetic word.

Your first job is to *get* the word or vision. Then your next job is to ask the Holy Spirit to interpret it. Keep in mind that He won't *always* interpret it for you. Remember the story at the beginning of the chapter? If you see a yellow shirt and He's not telling you what it means, you'll have to trust Him and take a risk. But I've found that the vast majority of the time, He'll give you the interpretation.

Okay, so you're looking at a blue car or you had a random thought about your Aunt Mary. Now you're going to ask the Holy Spirit what that means for the person you're getting a prophetic word for.

Just say in your mind, "Holy Spirit, what does that mean?" Then listen or watch for the interpretation. What generally happens for me is that suddenly the blue car image changes. Now, I see the blue car traveling down an 8-lane freeway that has no other cars on it. So I ask the Holy Spirit, "What does that mean? Is the fact that there are no other cars here relevant?" You can ask questions and press in to find answers. Prophecy is like a journey. The process of getting the word is fun and multi-layered. Most of the time, when you see a prophetic person doing this in front of a church congregation, they're going through all of this in their own head very quickly. They rarely verbalize the process out loud. You're doing the same thing right now but the process will probably take you more time at first.

If you're getting a prophetic word for your friend Susan when suddenly your Aunt Mary pops into your head for no logical reason, the Holy Spirit has dropped her into your imagination for a reason. Ask Him what's going on. Most likely, He wants you to notice something about Aunt Mary. As you think about her, suddenly you remember how much she loves gardening. Then as you picture her gardening, you suddenly see that whenever she plants a seed, it immediately springs up into a full-grown flower even before she's planted the next seed! What started off as a recollection suddenly turns into a prophetic vision! How'd that happen? Because you followed the Holy Spirit's lead.

So you tell your friend Susan that you see her (since Aunt Mary represents her) planting seeds that spring up immediately. Perhaps she is sowing seeds that she is able to immediately reap. Or maybe the Spirit is revealing to her that there is a supernatural acceleration coming on her ministry or her work. Ask Him what He means by that. Don't assume to know. Always give Him the first chance to interpret it. If He doesn't tell you, then just say what you see.

Often when I prophesy, it's like looking at static on a television. I start off with nothing. But as I watch the static, suddenly the static seems to briefly form an image. It's gone even before I can look closely. Was that my imagination? I'm immediately tempted to think it was. I usually have to consciously choose to believe it was the Holy Spirit. So I grab the image that I briefly saw and I reform it in my mind so I can see it clearly again.

I can't count the number of times that I've given a prophetic word from something as indistinct as this. At the moment I'm giving it, I'm 99.9% sure it's made-up and I'm about to give a wrong word. But it always turns out to be right! That's the "still, small voice of God." Getting and giving a prophetic word requires risk and faith, just like everything else in the Kingdom. If every prophetic word came in the form of a huge glowing neon sign and choirs of angels dancing around it, no faith would be required whatsoever. When we put our faith into action and we take a risk, God credits it to us as righteousness. Maybe He's giving us a way to build up treasures in heaven by making it a little bit harder. Whatever the reason, recognize that all of us with the gift of prophecy go through this. It's not just you! The more you practice this, the more confirmation you'll get. With confirmation comes confidence. And with confidence comes an assurance that you *are* hearing the voice of the Spirit, regardless of how it feels at the moment. I can tell you this from my own experience.

WHAT IF I FEEL LIKE I'M JUST MAKING IT UP?

Many times after giving a prophetic word, you may wonder if you just made it up. Because God often writes on the "whiteboard" of your imagination, your natural mind will assume you just made it up because it feels so similar. However, the prophetic word comes from the Holy Spirit and it often gets written into your imagination. Of course, you may have heard the word in other, more specific, ways. If you heard the word audibly inside your head, it may be so strong that you know for a fact it didn't come from you. But often, the prophetic word will come like a "still, small voice" that may seem almost indistinguishable from something you just made up. Nancy Cobb, a teacher of the prophetic gift at Bethel Church, says, "In your head, your 'Prophesier' is located really close to your 'Maker-Upper'."

Because of this, you may feel immediate doubt about the word you gave. The next time you have an opportunity to prophesy, you may feel less inclined to give the word since you may feel like you're making it up. And the enemy is going to be right there, trying to convince you of this so he can shut you down. Don't listen to it.

First, recognize that the feeling is normal and everyone experiences it during the early learning process! What you need is confirmation. Confirmation gives you a track record that lets you build up your faith in your own prophetic gifting so that, regardless of how you feel after giving a word to someone, you will know your own track record and you don't need to worry about it.

Establishing your own track record is important for you to become more confident in the prophetic gift. It is imperative that you have people with whom you can practice safely! Without practice, you may feel afraid to step out for fear of someone condemning your ability or you may afraid of giving an incorrect word to someone who doesn't know how to judge it properly. With a safe environment, you can feel comfortable giving prophetic words often. Through this type of repetitive practice, you will quickly realize that you are hearing from God as people confirm the words you are giving them.

The Importance of Confirmation

In a prophetic culture where everyone is prophesying over everyone else as often as possible, people will often receive the same words from others. As you practice prophesying, pretty soon you'll hear someone say, "Wow, I just got that word from someone else a couple days ago!" or "Hey, you just confirmed a word I got last month," or "God's been speaking to me about that today." Trust me, this will happen on a surprisingly regular basis. When you start hearing this from people, you're going to realize that you *are* hearing the prophetic voice of God even though it probably doesn't feel like it at the moment. You won't feel lightning bolts from heaven striking your spirit as you're giving a word. But hearing people confirm the word you just gave them is what you need to build up confidence in your prophetic gift. Remember, confirmation brings confidence!

Carrying the Prophetic Word

One of the purposes of prophecy is to build faith and to create in us an expectation for something that will happen. It can give us an ability to prepare for it, pray into it, earnestly expect it, and act out our faith toward the prophetic word.

Several years ago, I was visiting a church and went forward to receive prayer after the service. At one point, the person praying for me prophesied that God would be giving me dreams and that I was to keep a pen and paper by my bedside so I could write them down. I had never received a dream from God so I was very excited about this. Just a few days later, I was volunteering at a Christian television studio to help with some technical work. After the on-air show, one of the guests offered to prophesy over the volunteers. When she got to me,

PROPHECY

she said God would be giving me dreams and that I was to keep a pen and paper by my bedside. It was practically a word-for-word reproduction of the prophecy I'd received just a few days earlier, even though she didn't know me and knew nothing about my previous prophecy.

I had no doubt this was a prophetic word from God and that it was important enough that He gave it to me twice. I earnestly began expecting dreams from God. I kept a pen and paper by my bedside and waited.

Several months went by with no dreams from God. But still, I knew that He would give me what He had promises. I didn't know why I hadn't gotten any yet but I had no doubt that they would come. Sure enough, about three or four months after the prophetic words, I got my first dream from God. I wrote it down. Then a few months later, I got another one. And God kept giving me dreams on a regular (although infrequent) basis. As I began getting regular dreams, I started asking God to have them more frequently. I was thankful for the ones I was having, but I was desperate for more! I also looked around for people who didn't get prophetic dreams so I could impart the grace that God had given me. I knew that if I gave away what I had, God would give me even more.

These two prophecies in the same week served to build my faith and created an expectancy in me. I acted on my faith by making room for the prophetic word to happen. I kept a pen and paper by my bedside, knowing that I would need them when I woke up one morning (or in the middle of the night) after receiving a dream. I prayed into it, asking and believing God for the dreams He had promised. And I never lost hope. The prophecy was like fuel in my gas tank, allowing me to get to the destination where my dreams from God were waiting.

PREPARING THE WAY FOR THE PROPHETIC WORD TO BE MANIFEST

Prophetic words from God carry grace that allows people to come into the full realization of the prophetic word. This is part of the "forth-telling" aspect of prophecy. It isn't just an interesting word of information, meant only for the mind. The grace that God has put on the word carries the power to change the person.

But many forth-telling and fore-telling prophetic words need to be brought forth into existence. God has spoken something that is forming in you or that is coming in your future. You have the power to accelerate it by carrying it and preparing for it.

God could have given me prophetic dreams without first telling me He was going to do it. But I quite likely would have dismissed those dreams, as I did all the other "normal" ones I had. I didn't know that God had targeted me to have prophetic dreams. Once He told me, I was amazed and honored. I began to expect it. And by expecting it, I was analyzing every dream. As soon as I woke up from a dream, or as soon as I remembered a dream later in the day, I immediately considered it from a spiritual perspective to see if it was a dream from God. At first, none of my regular dreams stood out. They were the same. But then, a couple months after the prophetic words, I had my first dream from God. Because I was looking and waiting for it, I recognized it when it appeared! Without the prophetic word from God, I'm sure I would not have recognized it.

So one of God's purposes for revealing things through the gift of prophecy is to give us a "heads-up" for things coming into our lives soon. He gives us this heads-up so we'll expect and wait for it, like a friend that calls to let you know that he is visiting your city and will be dropping by at a specific date and time. Because you know, you will make sure you're home, your living room will be clean and presentable, and you'll be eagerly waiting for him.

What are some ways you can prepare for or carry a prophetic word until it is fully manifest?

First, you need to believe it. And as you know by now, belief is more than a thought. It requires action. So look at the prophetic word. How can you act on it? How can you draw power from it? How can you empower the grace that is already on it?

There was a woman who received a prophecy that she would be leading worship in the church. This woman had absolutely no musical talents or giftings. Before this prophecy, she had little desire for music because of her lack of talent. But after she heard this word, she decided to believe it. And then she acted on it. She believed she could receive grace from this prophetic word so that she could become a worship leader.

She began taking music and singing lessons and discovered that she did have a new talent which she didn't have before the prophecy. God gave her grace to become something she wasn't before. But she had to receive it by acting it out.

In just a couple years, this woman was indeed leading worship at her church.

Often, God is giving us a prophetic word about our future so that we can prepare for it and begin acting on it. When a couple takes a pregnancy test and finds out they're pregnant, they have just received the equivalent of a prophetic word. They know their future is about to change drastically. So what do they do with that "prophetic" word? They immediately begin preparations for the baby's arrival. They come up with ideas for a name, buy clothing and car seats, tell all their friends, buy photo albums, and maybe decorate and paint a nursery room. By the time the baby arrives, everything is ready for her. She can be cared for and nurtured because of those preparations. The baby's arrival doesn't cause chaos, confusion, and frustration. Instead, she brings joy.

WHY ISN'T PROPHECY PROMOTED IN THE CHURCH?

Prophecy has been despised and feared by parts of the church for a long time. In Numbers chapter 11, Moses told God that he was having trouble carrying the burden of all the people by himself. God answered Moses by telling him to find 70 elders of the people and to bring them to the Tent of Meeting. There, God would take His Spirit that was on Moses and He would also give it to the elders. Moses went and found 70 elders but only 68 showed up at the Tent of Meeting. Two others didn't come.

Of those gathered in the Tent, the Spirit rested on them and they prophesied. Interestingly, the other two that chose not to attend this meeting also received the same Spirit. Wherever they were in the camp, they also began to prophesy when the Spirit came upon them. This was reported to Moses, and Joshua said, "Moses, stop them!" The people were uncomfortable hearing from God through anyone other than Moses himself. But in Numbers 11:29, Moses replies, "Are you jealous for my sake? I wish that all the Lord's people were prophets and that the Lord would put his Spirit on them!"

I'm sure many pastors would agree that it can be challenging trying to be the "voice of God" for the entire congregation. But this is not biblical. In Acts 2, God fulfilled Moses' desire and He fulfilled the prophecy of Joel when He poured out His Spirit on all flesh. Now, anyone can hear from God directly! We can also hear the voice of God for other people so that we can speak it out to them. Moses wanted relief from the heavy burden of being the only leader for millions of Jews in the wilderness. Pastors and leaders wanting relief need only create a prophetic culture that allows God's voice to be easily accessible by anyone, anytime, anywhere, for anyone. On Pentecost, God answered Moses' prayer by pouring out His spirit so that now all the Lord's people can be prophets.

Some churches have had problems in the past with prophetic words that were given without proper boundaries that allowed it to flourish safely. Because of problems and messes, they chose to shut it down entirely or to limit it only to specific people who were known to prophesy safely and accurately. This is probably responsible for the Christian belief that "only certain people can prophesy and I'm not one of them." The apostle Paul's desire was for every believer to prophesy. That can happen, as long as safe boundaries are established and people are willing to clean up any messes or craters they leave behind from big mistakes. It also helps for people to know how to flush prophecies that are incorrect, inaccurate, or come from the wrong spirit (e.g., from the person and not from God). Being able to discern prophetic words is as essential as knowing how to prophesy. Ever believer should prophesy. Every believer should also practice the gift of discernment by testing and judging the prophetic word.

WHAT IF I ACCIDENTALLY GIVE A WRONG WORD?

The tendency for people to expect perfect words from prophets and people with the gift of prophecy is why the prophetic gift is often kept hidden away. If a prophetic person knows that someone might "kill the messenger" if they make a mistake, they're just going to clam up. For a prophetic culture to flourish, there needs to be grace, forgiveness, and love. It's a good thing these are core values for all Christians!

Consider this: In Deuteronomy 18:20, God commanded the people to put to death any prophet who spoke words that God did not command him to say. Why was that so important? Because God gave the Holy Spirit to prophets, but He did not give it to the people. The people were spiritually dead and had no ability to discern through the Spirit. The prophets *did* have the ability to hear very clearly from God so they knew what to say. The people, however, did not have the

Holy Spirit so they had no clear way to discern the source of the prophetic words.

Today, all Christians have (or should have!) the Holy Spirit. This gives them access to the gifts of the Spirit, including the gift of prophecy and the gift of discernment. Today, unlike those living under the old covenant, all Christians have the ability to discern the prophetic word and to judge whether it is from God or not. The Holy Spirit allows us to speak His words to others. The same Holy Spirit also allows us to judge and discern the word. Because we have the Holy Spirit, it is the responsibility of the receiving person to use the Holy Spirit to judge the word. If they immediately assume the word is from God when it may not necessarily be, that is their own fault and responsibility.

Every Holy Spirit-filled believer has access to the gift of discernment and the spirit of wisdom and revelation. As such, God expects every believer to use it. These gifts and abilities, combined with grace and love, is why we don't "kill the messenger" today.

What Do I Do With a Prophetic Word That Is Wrong?

If you receive a prophetic word that you believe is wrong through your gift of discernment, then you have done as Paul commanded when he said, "Do not despise prophetic utterances. But **examine everything carefully**; hold fast to that which is good." (1 Thes. 5:20-21 [NASB]) Also in 1 John 4:1, we are instructed to do the following: "Dear friends, do not believe every spirit, but test the spirits to see whether they are from God, because many false prophets have gone out into the world." A false prophet is not somebody who gives a wrong prophetic word! Don't condemn them. If they are still learning and practicing, give them a *lot* of grace. Be willing to receive another prophetic word from them because you have the ability to "test the spirits" and to flush anything that isn't healthy.

There are four sources of prophetic words. All sources originate in the spiritual realm, but not all originate from the Spirit of God. These sources are:

1. Our Spirit
2. The Holy Spirit
3. Evil Spirits
4. Angels

Notice that all four are spirits. As such, all four have the ability to speak in the spiritual realm in such a way that another spiritually-sensitive person (one with the gift of prophecy) can receive it. Although I've found it to be very unlikely, it is nevertheless possible that the prophetic word you received came from a source other than God. Does that make the person giving it a false prophet? Not necessarily. A false prophet is one who misuses the gift of prophecy to draw people to himself, rather than to God. He claims the glory that is meant for God.

We are to test the prophetic word and hold on to what is good. If part of a prophetic word seems wrong, does that invalidate the rest of the word that seems good? Paul says to "hold on that which is good" meaning that you should eat the meat and spit out the bones. Hopefully, we're only prophesying "meat" but occasionally a bone may sneak in. So just spit it out! This provides a safe, healthy prophetic culture where people are free to learn and grow as they practice the gift of prophecy and learn to hear the voice of the Spirit.

How to Judge a Prophetic Word

In order to safely receive prophetic words, you have a responsibility to judge them first. You don't have to automatically accept every prophetic word. Before accepting it, make sure it follows these Biblical principles:

- Does it glorify God? (John 16:14; 1 Corinthians 12:3; 1 John 4:1-2)

- Does it agree with God's word? (Isaiah 8:20)

- Do the person's previous prophecies bear good fruit or bad fruit? (Matthew 7:16-18,20)

- Do the prophecies produce liberty or bondage? (Romans 8:15)

- You have an anointing to discern the truth. The prophetic word should bear witness with your spirit. (1 John 2:20)

GROWING IN PROPHECY

As you're starting out with the gift of prophecy, it's like riding a bicycle for the first time. Scary and exhilirating. You just hope you don't fall off and scrape your knee. If it happens, you just brush off the dirt, stick a band-aid on it, and get back on the bike. That's the only way to get better.

If you've surrounded yourself with fellow "students" of the gifts of the Spirit, then you have a safe place to practice prophesy. The only way to grow is to practice and do it often. Set a goal: three prophetic words every day. Keep a journal of your experiences. How confident do you feel about the words you're giving? Have you gotten confirmations from people? If so, write these down!

As you practice and journal your experiences, you'll quickly notice that you're becoming better at hearing God's voice and seeing/sensing things in the spiritual realm. Remember, you bought this book to activate the spiritual gifts within you. So don't just read about prophecy. *Now it's time for you to do it!*

Chapter 9

WORDS *of* KNOWLEDGE

Words of knowledge are one of my favorite gifts of the Spirit. They are one of the most versatile and powerful gifts God can give us. A word of knowledge works with many of the other gifts in such a seamless way, but produces even more amazing results.

A word of knowledge is any information that the Holy Spirit reveals to you about another person that you couldn't have otherwise known. For example, you may be sitting next to somebody on a city bus and suddenly you know (through any of several possible ways) that the person has kidney disease and her kidneys are slowly dying. This is a word of knowledge. The Holy Spirit has revealed this to you so that you can release healing. Or perhaps you're sitting next to somebody on an airplane and the Holy Spirit is quiet. So you decide to go get a word of knowledge from Him. You open up your spirit, asking Him to reveal something about the person you're sitting next to. And suddenly, you sense that the man is both an artist and a construction worker. You're wondering which of the two it is since they seem so contradictory, but you decide to take a risk. So you ask him if he is a construction worker. And he says he sometimes works on home construction, but only when his ceramic art sculptures aren't selling.

A couple years ago, I first learned what a word of knowledge was. I'd heard of that term before but never knew what it really meant. When I realized that the Holy Spirit could reveal information to me about other people, I thought that was the most amazing thing I'd ever heard of! It was too good to be true. I'm a very logical person so I loved the idea that I could practice this and immediately know if I was right or wrong. There was no room for a gray area, so I'd have an easy benchmark as I practiced to see how I was doing. Sometimes with healings, the person may be partially healed. Sometimes with prophecy, you're not immediately sure about the prophetic word you're getting. Both take time to build confidence as you see a track record. But words of knowledge are instantly verifiable and I thought I could grow very quickly in it as a result.

I learned about words of knowledge from Kris Vallotton, one of the pastors at Bethel. Immediately after he taught us about them, he gave us the impartation of the gift. Then, he had us all stand and pair up with somebody else. He told us to get a word of knowledge about the other person. We were then instructed to give our word of knowledge to the other person, and they had to answer in only one of two ways: "Yes, that's correct," or "No, that's incorrect." There was no gray area. No "well, you're kind of right." Just yes or no. That was both terrifying and thrilling! Eagerly, I tried it out. And I was wrong! But I didn't feel quite so bad since about 95% of the class got theirs wrong, too.

For the next few months, I eagerly pursued this gift. I kept practicing with other students and I kept getting them wrong, over and over. I practiced it so many times, statistically I should have gotten at least one right simply by guessing! But no, I didn't even have that. Finally out of desperation, I was talking with another student who had taken this class a year earlier and had a good track record of words of knowledge. He gave me an amazing bit of advice: "Don't worry how many you get right or wrong, just keep going until you get it. And when you start getting one or two right, keep going until you get more right. Just keep going and you'll acquire it."

That helped rejuvenate my desire. I practiced words of knowledge with everyone I could. It became almost a running joke: instead of walking up to somebody at church and saying, "Hi," I would instead walk up and say, "Hey, can I practice a word of knowledge with you?" Sitting around a campfire with a dozen other Christians, we would spend an hour just practicing words of knowledge. "Does your car have 116,000 miles on it? No? Umm... was your first dog's name Eliza? No? Okay, is your middle name Eric? No?"

Of course, around the campfire others would get a few right and I was still getting shot down left and right. I was collecting "No's" like some people collect baseball cards. I didn't let it faze me. Then suddenly, two or three months after I started, I got my first one right! It blew me away! There was a temptation from the enemy to think that it was just a lucky guess. But I pushed that thought aside and thanked God for the word of knowledge I'd just received. Then I asked Him for even more! I knew there was more and I pursued it even harder. I practiced words of knowledge with others even more.

Over the next few months, I began to get about one word of knowledge correct for every six or eight attempts. But as I kept practicing it, I got better and better. Soon, I was getting one right for every five or six.

It was somewhere around this time that I heard conference speaker Bobby Conner give an amazing testimony of a word of knowledge during one of his conference sessions. He told us about a conference he was speaking at where there was a very distinguished-looking man sitting in the back row of the church. The man had his arms folded and looked incredibly skeptical of everything happening in the church service that night. At some point in the evening, Bobby asked the man to come up to the front because God was going to tell him something. The man walked up to the front, his body language still giving off skeptical vibes.

Bobby placed one hand on the man's shoulders and looked him in the eyes for a few seconds, and the man's gaze never left Bobby's. He was confident in his skepticism. Bobby said, "What do these numbers mean to you?" and he began rattling off a long string of numbers, something like 9-1-5-2-2-0-6-4-3-7. All of the sudden, this man got completely unhinged. He shouted, "Whoa!" in complete surprise. After a few seconds, he said to Bobby, "There is no possible way you could have known that."

Bobby asked excitedly, "Well, what do the numbers mean?"

The man said that many years earlier, he had been an undercover CIA operative. The numbers represented his operative number, something that was known by only two people on earth: him and his immediate supervisor. There was no way Bobby could have known the man's operative number except through a divine revelation in the form of a word of knowledge.

When I heard this testimony, I realized the kind of accuracy and detail that were possible with words of knowledge. I wanted it!

I kept practicing words of knowledge for months. Then during the summer, a friend and I went on a cruise in the Bahamas. During dinner one evening, I was practicing words of knowledge at the table without telling anyone else. I noticed the necklace one girl was wearing and asked her if it was a gift from her family. She said her dad had bought it for her. Then I noticed the earrings worn by her friend and asked if she had bought that just before the cruise because she wanted something new and nice to wear. She said, she had bought them about a week prior to the cruise. Then after the dinner, I asked one of our waiters (who was from Colombia) if he had a wife and three children at home. He said yes and proudly starting tell me all about them including their ages and what they were interested in.

As I walked back to my cabin, I thanked God for the level that I was at. I was honestly grateful that words of knowledge had become so easy. And yet, I was still hungry for the "Bobby Conner" level! I knew I could get there. So I reminded Him that I wanted to be at that level and I asked Him to help me get there.

The next evening at dinner, I had totally forgotten about this prayer. As I was eating my dessert, I was absent-mindedly scanning the room and people-watching. I noticed one of our waitresses about 30 feet away helping another table. The only thing I knew about her is that her name was Agnieszka. As I watched her, suddenly this thought flashed into my head in an instant: Agnieszka is saving up all of her cruise ship income to open up a bar-restaurant in Poland and it's been her dream for a long time. It flashed into my head so quickly, I realized I couldn't have made it up. But I also knew that I never got such detailed and specific words of knowledge! I was in a quandary. Now what should I do? Luckily, my friend (who is also a revivalist) was sitting next to me at the table. So I told him about this. But I wasn't very confident in the details so I intentionally didn't say "in Poland" because Agnieszka's name sounded Russian or maybe Ukrainian. I was sure it was wrong.

When I told him the information, he said, "How do you know, did she tell you that?" I said, "No, I think it might be a word of knowledge." He said, "So, are you going to ask her about it?"

I pondered that for a moment. I wasn't thrilled at the thought of being wrong with something so specific but I really wanted to know! So I said, "Yes, I'll ask her when she comes back around to our table."

About five minutes later, she came back and was standing next to me so I looked up at her and said, "Agnieszka, are you saving up your cruise ship income to open a bar-restaurant, and has it been your dream to do so?"

She just stood there looking at me for about three full seconds, then she slapped me in the shoulder good-naturedly and said loudly, "Yeah! How did you know that?!"

Right then, I remembered that all cruise ship employees have their home country listed on their name tags. I squinted up at hers and read the word "Poland."

I told her that God had revealed this information to me because He loved her dream and He wanted to bless it and help her succeed in it. She was very honored to know that God had supernaturally revealed her dream to someone else so that she could know how much God knows the secrets of her heart. She had not told anyone else on the ship this secret dream of hers. She knew it was absolutely miraculous and she gladly accepted my offer of a prayer of blessing on her idea and on her future business.

I have spent a lot of time on this personal testimony because it encompasses so many things I want you to learn. This story shows you my hunger and faith. I knew I could have the gift of words of knowledge. I was desperately hungry for it. I knew it would be an amazing tool of evangelism. I knew that unsaved people who are yearning to believe in a supernatural God and who are desperate for some kind of radical encounter with Him needed a word of knowledge. I knew I could offer it to them if I could not only acquire it, but if I could grow in it. I had faith that I would have it and I never wavered from it (although I definitely had a frustrating couple of months before I got the first one right). If you really want something, if you're really hungry for it, nothing will stop you from getting it except your own hunger level.

As you read my testimony, you may have bristled when you read about how we would sit around a campfire and seemingly play with the gift as if it were a toy. Asking the Holy Spirit for the number of miles on a car? The name of a person's first dog? That won't get anyone saved, healed or delivered, right? Are we disrespecting the Holy Spirit when we do this?

No, not at all. Paul instructed Timothy to "practice these things, devote yourself to them, so that all may see your progress" (1 Timothy 4:15). We were practicing the gift of words of knowledge and we devoted ourselves to it, so that we would make progress in our growth and use of the gift.

By practicing the gift like this, first of all we were taking ownership of it. We made it our own. We made it a part of ourselves, like a sword becomes an extension of a soldier's arm who spends five hours a day practicing with it. As students, we wanted the gifts of the Spirit to become a part of our daily lifestyle. Of course we're going to have fun with it because God is fun and He delights in seeing us enjoy His gifts, just as a father delights in seeing his daughter enjoy a new bicycle he purchased for her. He is going to love watching her spend hours riding it around in the neighborhood every day. If she only pulled it out once a week and rode it for five or six minutes, he'd have every right to wonder whether she really liked her gift.

JESUS AND THE WORD OF KNOWLEDGE

Jesus got words of knowledge which are recorded on a regular basis throughout the gospels. In John 4, He was talking to a woman at a well in Samaria while his disciples went off to buy food.

> *He told her, "Go, call your husband and come back."*
>
> *"I have no husband," she replied.*
>
> *Jesus said to her, "You are right when you say you have no husband. The fact is, you have had five husbands, and the man you now have is not your husband. What you have just said is quite true."*
>
> *"Sir," the woman said, "I can see that you are a prophet." (John 4:16-19)*

Jesus had never met this woman but knew something about her through a word of knowledge. The woman was immediately able to recognize God's grace on His life because of this amazing gift.

Jesus also got an accurate word of knowledge about Nathanael in John 1:47-50. Philip was called to be a disciple. Then he ran to tell Nathanael the good news that the Messiah had come, known as Jesus of Nazareth. Nathanael was skeptical, saying, "Nazareth! Can anything good come from there?" But Philip told him, "Come and see!"

> *When Jesus saw Nathanael approaching, he said of him, "Here is a true Israelite, in whom there is nothing false."*
>
> *"How do you know me?" Nathanael asked.*
>
> *Jesus answered, "I saw you while you were still under the fig tree before Philip called you."*
>
> *Then Nathanael declared, "Rabbi, you are the Son of God; you are the King of Israel."*
>
> *Jesus said, "You believe because I told you I saw you under the fig tree. You shall see greater things than that."*

The word of knowledge that Jesus got was simple but powerful. In His spirit, He saw Nathanael under the fig tree although he hadn't been physically present. It was exactly the confirmation that Nathanael needed to believe that Jesus was the Messiah, the prophesied Son of God. We who are disciples of Jesus now have access to the same calling card, the same proof that we have been sent by God.

OUR SUPERNATURAL CALLING CARD

When we make the gifts of the Spirit part of our daily lifestyle, we can get words of knowledge for anyone anywhere, regardless of whether the Holy Spirit is trying to tell us or not. Sometimes He's talking and you'll hear it, but other times you need to go get a word of knowledge. Just because He isn't speaking it out to you doesn't mean

He won't give you one if you ask Him. You are a co-laborer with the Holy Spirit. Sometimes He'll give you one before you even think to ask. Sometimes you'll need to ask and you'll get one.

In this instance of the woman at the well, Jesus used the word of knowledge as a supernatural way to reveal to her that He was the Son of God. The word of knowledge was like his business card that identified Him as an authorized representative of the kingdom. We who are also sons and daughters of God can have the exact same business card. When other people see this business card, they will also recognize the grace and power that is on our lives. How else could we have possibly known something about them unless God Himself revealed it to us? What an awesome gift this is! The world wants to know that God knows them. They want to know that God knows the secret desires of their heart. They want a supernatural demonstration of the power of the Living God. You are a walking demonstration of God's power. Words of knowledge are a fantastic way to give people an encounter with God.

Many times when I prophesy, I will find out later from the person I'm ministering to that some accurate words of knowledge were mixed in. Why and how? I didn't intend to because I usually don't realize it until the person tells me afterward. I've found that God likes to speak to people in their own language, as part of the "calling card" analogy. It's an easy way for God to underline the prophetic word by saying, "And just to prove that this is for you, the person prophesying over you who has never met you before will tell you things about yourself he couldn't possibly know."

One time, I was prophesying to a man and I saw an image of him working on power lines. I then proceeded to get an interpretation of the power lines which I spoke over him. Later, he came up to me and said, "You know, it's amazing. We've never met but you spoke to me in the language of my job. I'm an electrical lineman."

Another time, I prophesied over a young woman and I felt like she had written a letter to God when she was five or six years old. I also felt like she put it in an envelope and placed it under her pillow so God would read it. I told her these things although I was very unsure whether this was accurate or not, but decided to take a big risk by faith. As I told her this, I felt God telling me it was true and that I should continue. So without waiting for confirmation, I told her God's response to her childhood letter. As I spoke God's response, she was very emotionally moved. When we were finished, she said that she had indeed done what I had described through the word of knowledge. Here, God gave me this word of knowledge because He wanted to give her His response.

When I first pursued the gift of words of knowledge, I was pursuing it intentionally and I began to see results in my "practice sessions." But then later, I saw the fruit forming in my life. On a cruise ship, I get an "accidental" word of knowledge I wasn't even looking for. While prophesying, I will sometimes get words of knowledge without looking for them. I initiated my pursuit of this gift, God honored it, and now He has incorporated it into my lifestyle and my personal ministry. Just like a child needs to intentionally learn to ride a bike, spending a lot of time focusing on it, learning how to stay upright, how to turn corners without falling over, and how to stay on the seat without falling off, pretty soon her efforts will result in a learned skill. She will be able to successfully ride a bike without training wheels, and most importantly, without having to consciously think about it! Learning and practicing the spiritual gifts work much the same way. There is a learning period that only lasts for a season, although we still look for ways to move to the next level!

WORDS OF KNOWLEDGE FOR HEALING

It is possible to get a word of knowledge for someone's pain, sickness or disease. Obviously, this is useful so you can know what they need healing for. The purpose of this kind of word of knowledge is to cue you into something so that you can take the next logical step which is to release healing.

There are various ways you can get this kind of word of knowledge but the most common way is to feel a pain in your body that wasn't there a moment ago and which disappears within a few seconds. It is there long enough for you to shift your awareness to that portion of your body so you know there is somebody in your vicinity who needs to be healed. The interesting thing about this word of knowledge is that it can come on you without you even thinking to ask for it. Suddenly you feel a brief sharp pain in your stomach and then it's gone. Was that your lunch? Or was it a word of knowledge?

Start by asking the person closest to you if they have any pain or problems in their stomach or abdomen. There could be any of 30 different possible problems in the stomach area. It may have nothing to do with the stomach itself. Maybe somebody punched them in the stomach and it's hurting like crazy? You never know! So ask people around you, "Does anyone have pain in your stomach or any other kind of stomach problem?"

Someone may have no pain but they may have cancer in their abdomen. It won't always be pain that the word of knowledge is trying to point out to you. It could be a sickness or disease in that particular region of someone's body.

Next time you feel a sudden pain or tickling in a part of your body that seems out of place, try asking those around you if they need healing for anything in that part of their body. You'll be absolutely amazed how often this works!

Most often, I get words of knowledge for healing through my sanctified imagination. I give over my imagination to the Holy Spirit and let Him use it as a white board. When He draws things on it, I can see it very clearly. This (for me and many others) is the easiest way to get a word of knowledge or a prophecy. You'll find that prophecy and words of knowledge both come in similar ways because the gifts are very similar but they serve different purposes.

When I go looking for a word of knowledge, like when I go looking for a prophecy, I give over my imagination to the Holy Spirit. Then I watch to see what shows up there.

Sometimes I may see a picture. Other times it's a brief movie. Sometimes the person I'm looking at suddenly reminds me of somebody else although there isn't any logical reason why. Or maybe I suddenly remember some fact or object that has no connection with the person.

All of these are valid ways of getting words of knowledge, in exactly the same way as prophecy.

The only way to test a word of knowledge is to try it out. But don't walk around saying, "God just told me that your parent's names are Abigail and Eddie." If you're wrong, you're going to have an interesting mess to clean up. Instead, try this: "Are your parent's names Abigail and Eddie?" If you're wrong, it's no big deal. If you're right, they'll probably say something like, "Yes, why, do you know them?" Now you can tell them that God revealed it to you through the Holy Spirit. Or you can stay silent about it as you're simply practicing hearing the words of knowledge.

It helps to always phrase words of knowledge in the form of question, just like on Jeopardy. But here if you get it wrong, you won't have to worry about a smug host happily gloating as he tells you the correct response. Words of knowledge are easy and fun to practice because if you get them wrong, it's no big deal! If you walk up to somebody buying popcorn at the movie theater and say, "Hey, do you drive a Toyota Camry?" and he says no, it's not a problem. If he asks you why, you can shrug it off with, "Oh nothing, I was just wondering." But if he says something like, "Yeah, did I leave my lights on?" then you'll know you got it right! Words of knowledge are really easy to practice and become experienced in. And they're a LOT of fun.

The best and easiest way to practice words of knowledge is to get a safe group of people (church members, family, roommates, a home group, etc) and practice them often. Soon, you're going to find that you're getting them right a lot more than not. And soon, you'll find you're getting more details. Most often, the reason we don't get specific details is because we assume that the details we're seeing or getting are our imagination so we push them out of our imagination until we get something that feels "spiritual". As you're practicing with people in a safe environment, work hard not to push aside anything that comes into your imagination! You need to intentionally test that stuff out so you know what is you and what isn't. But you'll be surprised to discover that what feels like "you" is actually the Holy Spirit! It feels like it's just you because it's coming through your imagination and your natural mind has a rational, logical explanation: you made it up. But, as prophetic teacher Nancy Cobb says while she points at her head, "Your Prophesier is located *really close* to your Maker-Upper." Same thing with words of knowledge. You're probably going to feel like you're making it up. But you are intentionally giving your imagination over to the Holy Spirit and asking Him to speak to you through it. So you need to believe that He is the source of that information, not your imagination. The only way to know for sure is to test it out often until you have seen enough confirmation that you don't even worry about it anymore! That's why you need to practice it often. You're training your mind to stop rejecting things that feel like "you" because you've seen so often that it originated in the mind of the Holy Spirit, not your own mind.

Okay, try this exercise: Find somebody right now. I don't care if you know them or not. I don't care if you're reading this at a fast-food restaurant. Pick somebody behind the counter who looks bored. Now ask the Holy Spirit to give you a word of knowledge for them. Now check your imagination. Check your body. Is anything different? Is there a thought, picture, or recollection in your mind that wasn't there a moment ago? Did it seem to come out of nowhere?

Okay, good. Now go ask the person a question. Remember, asking it in the form of a question is a safe way to practice! So do it right now.

Were you right? If so, congratulations! It's that easy. Don't forget to thank God for the gift of words of knowledge. Now keep practicing! Use it often.

Okay, so for the other 95% of you who got it wrong, don't worry about it. You will get these right and you'll be so addicted to it, you won't be able to stop! You've just got to keep pursuing it and learning how to hear the voice of the Spirit. Most likely, your own mind is getting in the way of the Holy Spirit's voice. That's why it takes persistence and faith so that you can keep pursuing this until you get it, like a child learning to ride a bike. It takes time to train the brain muscles until it comes naturally. Everyone can learn to ride a bike. And everyone can get words of knowledge from the Holy Spirit, including you. Yes, you.

But just the fact that you tried it right now is a success. You took a risk! Congratulations! Now, ask God how proud He is of you. Did you feel that? That was His pride for you. He is so pleased with you right now, He can barely keep His composure! In fact, I think He's crying tears of joy. There you go, you pleased God. That wasn't so hard, was it?

As you continue practicing words of knowledge, you will find that you'll get them without realizing it. Often when I prophesy over someone, I'll get a word of knowledge mixed in. You may get them while you're just casually conversing with somebody. This has happened to me a number of times. The Holy Spirit lives in you. Who knows when and how He will suddenly speak up? Sometimes He works through you without you even knowing it because you've submitted yourself to His will and allowed yourself to be used.

Chapter 10

HEALING

"I command all pain to leave this man's body in the name of Jesus. Pain, you have no authority here. I release the healing power of Jesus to flow through him and bring restoration. No more pain."

I had my hands on the older man's shoulders as I and two other prayer team members released healing through the Holy Spirit. For the last seven years, he'd had nearly constant pain in his chest and neck. He described the pain in his chest as being like "pinched nerves" although he didn't know the cause of it.

After I spoke the words of faith and declaration over him, I asked him what he felt in his body.

"The pain is slightly gone," he said.

"How much is 'slightly'?" I asked.

"Maybe 5% gone," he replied.

We prayed again. First, we thanked God for the 5% miracle we'd seen, then we released more of the healing power of God into the man's body.

When we again asked how he felt, he said there was no change whatsoever.

No change. No change?! How was that possible? That was a frustrating moment.

For a few seconds, I thought about giving up and moving on to the next person. Maybe the next one would be easier to heal. But then I realized how dishonoring that was. This man had come to us expecting a supernatural encounter with the Holy Spirit that lives within us and clothes us with power. Was I here just to get another checkmark on my "testimony sheet" or was I here to give this man the encounter and the healing he needed?

I decided to ask the Holy Spirit why he wasn't being healed.

I didn't hear any response in my mind but I did have my eyes open as I asked the Holy Spirit. After about ten seconds of asking and waiting for an answer, I got an answer. As I was looking at the man's chest, for just a single brief instant, I saw (in my sanctified imagination) what looked like cactus or porcupine quills sticking in the man's chest. I saw at least 50 or 60 of them!

I asked the Holy Spirit what they were. Before He answered me, He revealed something else to me. At that moment, I could sense a leadership authority on the man. I didn't have any idea who he was (we were ministering at another church) but I felt like he was a church leader. I asked the gentleman and he said he was a leader in a satellite branch of this church we were in.

I asked the Holy Spirit what this information had to do with the quills sticking in his chest.

He showed me in my imagination, through the gift of prophecy, an image of this man standing in front of a group of people. He had a protective pose as he stood in front of them. He was facing away from them with his hands outstretched. In front of him was an army of enemy soldiers. He was standing between the army and the people behind who he was protecting. I could see the enemy launching arrows and spears at his "flock" but he was standing in front of them. For the last seven years, he was able to protect his people from the attacks but he'd ended up with many wounds in the chest of his spiritual body. The wounds were manifesting in his physical body as pain.

I told him what I saw and what the Holy Spirit was revealing to me. Then I told him that I wasn't going to pray. I was simply going to do a prophetic act that would release healing. I was going to remove the quills from his chest in the spiritual realm by doing the physical act in the natural realm. Physical obedience brings spiritual release. The Holy Spirit had given me the key to this man's healing.

I opened the eyes of my spirit so I could see the quills in his chest again. When I could see them clearly, I simply began to pluck them out. I started out slowly at first, picking them out one by one and tossing them on the floor. But then my hand moved faster and faster. The interesting thing is that each time I plucked a quill out, the man (whose eyes were closed during this time) would react physically. To me, it appeared that he could *feel* each quill being removed from him! I plucked them out faster and faster as the Holy Spirit directed my hands. I could see the spiritual realm superimposed over the natural realm and I watched my hands plucking out each quill until, after about 45 seconds or a minute, I pulled out the last one and tossed it on the floor. The entire time, the man shook violently as I removed each one.

Now, I could see that there were small red pock marks where the quills had been. I simply placed my hand on his chest. I didn't feel the need to say anything. I just held it there. I could feel the healing power of Jesus flow through my hand into his chest, as if a healing "salve" or ointment was being applied to him. After a few seconds, I felt in my spirit that I was done and that he was free of pain.

I asked him how he felt.

"It's incredible! I could actually feel you remove each one! The pain became less and less as you kept removing them. Now, all of the pain is completely gone! Even my neck pain is totally gone. I haven't felt this good in years!"

In the last couple of years that I've been really going after supernatural healing by the power of God, I've encountered many people who just don't seem to get healed. It's always been frustrating for me. Is it because God doesn't want to heal them? Is it because their faith isn't great enough? Is my faith not great enough?

I've since learned, through teaching, through experience, and from the Holy Spirit, that the answer to those three questions is "no." The reason, as the Holy Spirit has been showing me, is often because we aren't partnering with Him properly. We live in an "instant" culture: instant coffee, fast food, on-demand television and movies, and high-speed Internet. Not all healings are instantaneous. Sometimes, we need to press through and ask the Holy Spirit, "What's going on? What should I do next?" Just a simple question like that is the key that opens up a whole new room in the healing realm. As you use the gift of prophecy to "see" or feel in the spiritual realm, you'll be amazed at the strategies Jesus gives you to release the healing. And you'll notice that no prayer was required for the man's healing. It was simply a partnership with Jesus. He wanted to release healing more than any of us wanted it. But He needed us to do a physical, prophetic act of faith that would release it. Physical obedience brings spiritual release. We didn't have to pray, "Oh God, please heal this man! Have mercy on your servant. Jesus died for this man to be healed. Please heal him right now!" We didn't plead, beg or beseech. We already knew the victory of Jesus is complete. His victory was not only over sin, but over sickness, pain, disease, and death.

All we had to do was live in our identity as "co-laborers" with God. By doing so, He was able to work with us to bring the healing that Jesus provided in his death and resurrection.

Does God Want To Heal Every Person?

Up until a few years ago, I took note of the fact that not everybody got healed. I honestly believed that God healed people. I had seen God heal some people before (though never through me, at the time). I knew divine healing was Biblical. But I tried to make logical sense of two apparent facts: 1) God heals, and 2) Not everyone gets healed. My logical mind demanded an answer to this quandary. All I could come up with was this stupid lie that I believed: God *can* heal everyone, but He doesn't always *choose* to.

My first mistake was allowing my natural, unrenewed mind to have any part of this process. My spiritual mind, the renewed mind of Christ that is within me, knew the truth: God wants to heal everyone! But my logical mind didn't see evidence of that. So I allowed my natural mind to dominate my thinking because I believed the inferior evidence of the natural realm in which I didn't see everyone get healed.

Colossians 3:2 reminds us to "set your mind on things above, not on earthly things." I also needed to "walk by faith, not by sight," as II Cor. 5:7 tells us. There is a reason why we are called believers who walk by faith. Regardless of what our physical eyes tell us, we have to believe that God's promises are true. Always. There are no asterisks next to His promises along with a lot of disclaimers written in small type at the bottom of the page. His promises are true. It was I who made the critical mistake: I wasn't walking by faith, and I wasn't setting my mind on things above.

Does God want to heal everyone? Absolutely yes. How can I be so sure?

God said to the Israelites in Exodus 15:26, "I will put none of these diseases on you for I am the Lord that heals you (Jehovah Rapha)." One of God's names is Jehovah Rapha, the Lord who heals. When God reveals a name for Himself, He does this to indicate one of His unfailing characteristics. He never revoked this name which means He never revoked this quality. Jesus is the same yesterday, today and forever. Jehovah Rapha is still our Healer today, just as He was when He revealed this to the Israelites in the Bible and just like when He manifested this quality through Jesus.

Do you believe salvation from sin is available through the atonement of Jesus? Do you believe we can be saved from our sins through our faith in Jesus as we accept Him into our heart? Okay, since you believe that, then it's just as important to understand that healing of sickness is also provided in the atonement.

The death and resurrection of Jesus didn't just give us freedom from sin and eternity in heaven. God also provided for the healing of people's bodies. This is revealed in Psalm 103:2-3, in which David states, "Praise the Lord, O my soul… who forgives all your sins and heals all your diseases." And 1 Peter 2:24 says, "He himself bore our sins in his body on the tree, so that we might die to sins and live for righteousness; by his wounds you have been healed." Isaiah 53:5 also speaks of this. Forgiveness of sin and healing of diseases are inextricably linked together in the amazing blood of Jesus. Why is that?

It started with the fall of man in the Garden of Eden. Their sin cost them a lot: it brought corruption into the world which caused the ground to be less productive, brought pain, sickness, disease, death, and separation from the presence of God. It also gave our authority to Satan which is what he was looking for as he was tempting them.

Jesus came to earth as the second Adam to right the mistakes of the first. He came to live a sinless life so He could regain the keys of authority over the earth. He came to provide a way for us to experience the presence of God in an intimate way once again, so that we could once again "walk with the Lord in the cool of the evening" as Adam and Eve had done. Salvation from our sin allows us to walk in this intimate relationship. But also, Jesus came to bring us freedom from the corruption of the world which brought sickness and disease. This is why He went around healing the sick everywhere He went. He was showing them that what had been lost in the Fall of Man had now been restored. No longer did we live under the curse of sin. Now, we had freedom from all aspects of the curse. No more separation from God the Father. No more shame or guilt from sin. No more pain. No more sickness or disease. Once again, man had authority over the earth. Jesus Himself regained this authority. And then He gave the keys of authority to us! This is why He commanded His disciples to "heal the sick" in Matthew 10:8. He was showing them that they once again had authority over the curse of sin, but there was a lawbreaker who was not ready to hand over his authority without a fight. We are to take dominion over the earth, over the curse of sin, and to reclaim the territory that is currently under enemy control. We now have complete authority to reclaim it. We just need to go do it!

The Israelites were given the Promised Land. But what did they find when they got there? The enemy was camped there in strongholds. They had to go clear out the squatters. We have been given a Promised Land: the kingdom of heaven established on earth. We are commanded to pray and do the following thing: "Father, your kingdom come, your will be done, on earth as it is in heaven."[1] We are not just to pray this but to *do* this. We've been given the power and authority through the Holy Spirit. Now, we just need to follow through. Yes, there will be some enemy encampments. They won't want to leave. But we have all authority because Jesus said, "All authority in heaven and on earth has been given to me. Therefore go!"[2]

We already believe every person can be saved from their sin. God doesn't turn some people down. We know He saves everyone who comes to Him. In the same way that salvation is for everyone, we must also believe that healing is for everyone.

Jesus healed all who came to Him. He never turned anyone down. He didn't say to them, "Sorry, it's my Father's will that you have this disease because it's building character in you. Now buck up, go home, and enjoy your suffering." No, He healed them *every* time.

We know that the curse of sin brought sickness and diseases into the world. We also know that the devil oppresses people with sickness and disease.

Acts 10:38 says, "How God anointed Jesus of Nazareth with the Holy Spirit and with power, and went about doing good and healing all who were oppressed by the devil, for God was with Him." And John 10:10 says, "the thief comes to steal, kill and destroy." He is a lawbreaker but we have authority to take back what he has stolen. The Holy Spirit gives us His restoring power so we can undo what the enemy has destroyed. And we have the resurrection power to raise the dead who were killed unnecessarily by the enemy. Doesn't this make you thrilled to be a Christian? It does for me! This is so much more fun than going to church every Sunday wondering if that's all that's available in my Christian life.

Now that I know my identity in God and I realize that I have the same Holy Spirit in me that Jesus had, I am walking in my destiny. The sick are being healed through the power of the Holy Spirit in me. You have the exact same destiny. There is nothing fundamentally different between me and you. I'm no more special than you. God doesn't favor me more. That's why I'm teaching you the keys that will unlock healing rooms of destiny that await you. God's healing power wants to flow through you to His people.

You don't need to convince God of your desire for the gift of healing because *He is trying to convince you of His desire for you to have it!*

THE IMPORTANCE OF TESTIMONIES

Whether a healing seems great (cancer disappearing) or small (headache disappearing), it all requires the exact same healing power of the Holy Spirit. We can't classify things in such a way that we only thank God or rejoice for "great" healings. From God's vantage point, they are all the same. It is only from a human perspective that we would consider the healing of pain in a person's pinky finger to be a "small" healing compared to a paralyzed person getting up out of a wheelchair and walking for the first time.

We must rejoice over any kind of healing, regardless of what it is, and regardless of whether the healing came through our hands or through someone else. Healings are a manifestation of God's glory. We should always have a heart of thankfulness whenever God shows up, in whatever way He shows up.

If you are in a church body or a home group that is seeking after healings and one occurs through another person, you may feel a temptation to be jealous or to be discouraged. Honestly, I'll say that temptation comes to me sometimes. But I'm here to tell you… don't be jealous and don't be discouraged! Instead, be honestly thankful that God is honoring your church or home group's call to manifest His glory. Be thankful for the miracle and rejoice!

Remember, the gifts of the Spirit are not a badge of honor or an award for "good behavior" on a particular person. If you are hearing a testimony and you experience the temptation to feel discouraged, recognize that it *is* a temptation and put it off. Refuse it. Actively get rid of it, then do the opposite. Be encouraged! God is showing up in power.

As everyone in your group continues to pursue God and His kingdom, more and more such testimonies will happen. Before you know it, you will be testifying of something that happened through you. God works in groups, he requires honor, and he loves a thankful heart. Be careful with your attitude because it's easy to slip into dangerous territory if you're not aware of this.

Also remember that public testimonies are not like elementary school show-and-tell. I remember show-and-tell as an opportunity to be really jealous of someone else's amazing new toy. When I went home, suddenly my own toys weren't good enough. To some people, public testimonies may be pressing buttons in you that you didn't even know were still there. Remember the purpose of testimonies: to bring glory and fame to the name of Jesus, to encourage and build up the body of Christ, to challenge and inspire others to also pursue the same thing, and especially, to build up faith. If one person could do it, so can everyone else!

Whenever you hear a testimony, take a few seconds and imagine yourself doing exactly what they did. By imagining it, you've made it real to yourself. You've taken ownership. Now, it's no longer their testimony, it's also yours. This enables you to repeat what has already happened once. God doesn't want things done just once. He wants to continue doing them through all of His body. Jesus came to earth to be the ultimate model. He is the testimony, and we are expected to repeat what He did the first time.

THE RIVER OF LIFE

In the Law of Moses, God had strict commands regarding those with leprosy. They were "unclean" and were not allowed to be touched because leprosy spreads by physical contact. If anyone touched a leper, they also became unclean. Contrast this with the New Testament where Jesus healed lepers by touching them. The lepers didn't make Jesus unclean because "Greater is He that is in Me than he that is in the world."[3]

The power of the Holy Spirit in Jesus was greater than the curse of leprosy or sickness in others that he touched. So instead of being infected by them, His purity and life actually infected them and affected them positively. We must realize that the Holy Spirit *within* us is life that can flow out *from* us. We can release that life through faith (believing that the hoped-for result will really happen) and through the laying-on of hands.

The Holy Spirit can flow through us with life-giving power because it is a "river of life." We see this river flowing out from the throne of the temple mentioned in both Ezekiel and Revelation.

In Ezekiel 47:1, we read about this river:

The man brought me back to the entrance of the temple, and I saw water coming out from under the threshold of the temple toward the east (for the temple faced east). The water was coming down from under the south side of the temple, south of the altar.

And in verse 9, we see its effect on the salty sea into which it flows:

Swarms of living creatures will live wherever the river flows. There will be large numbers of fish, because this water flows there and makes the salt water fresh; so where the river flows everything will live.

Where the river flows, everything will live. Our bodies are a temple of God. The Holy Spirit dwells in the temple of our body. As John 7:38 tells us, "Whoever believes in me... streams of living water shall flow from within him." This river of living water makes salty waters fresh so that everything can live. Salt is considered corruption of pure water but the river of living water makes it fresh, pure, and able to sustain life. In fact, verse 12 of Ezekiel 47 talks about the trees of life that grow along the banks of this river and says that "their fruit will serve for food and their leaves for healing." This prophetic vision is also described in Revelation 22:1-2.

This is how Jesus was able to touch the leper and make him clean. This is how the woman with the issue of blood was able to crawl her way through the crowd and touch His garment so she could be healed. She knew that a river of living water flowed from Him. All she had to do was make a connection so that it could flow into her body. When it did, she received the healing waters. This same river of living, healing water exists inside of us in the form of the Holy Spirit, waiting to be released through our faith in action.

Jesus commanded us to "Heal the sick, cleanse the lepers, raise the dead, cast out demons. Freely you have received, freely give." We have freely received the living water. Now we are commanded to give it away. A river must flow, otherwise it will become stagnant. We must allow the river to flow so it remains fresh. It must have an inlet and an outlet. We must be constantly being filled with the Holy Spirit so we can give Him away. And we must constantly give Him away so we can once again be filled. This is the river of life.

A Scriptural Theology of Healing

There are many wonderful books that describe the theology of healing in great detail. Rather than fill up this book with all those details, I've summarized the basic theology of healing so you can read and learn on your own.

- Exodus 15:26 Old Testament promise of healing. Jehovah Rapha, "The Lord Who Heals"
- Isaiah 53:4-5 Healing is in the atonement. The atonement covers: grief and sorrow; physical affliction; transgressions; and sin
- Matthew 8:16-17 states that it's a fulfillment of Isaiah 53
- 1 Peter 2:24 Sins forgiven and physical healing
- 1 Thess. 5:23 Sanctify completely, spirit/soul/body
- Luke 5:17-24 Story of four friends and a paralyzed man. "Which is easier to say, Your sins are forgiven you or rise up and walk?"
- James 5:14-15 Sickness and sin healed
- Luke 5:12-13 "Lord, if you are willing, you can make me clean." Jesus replies, *"I am willing."* It is always His will to heal.
- The Greek word for "saved" is *sozo* which means "saved, healed, delivered and made whole". It's a body, soul, and spirit salvation which includes more than sins. It also includes physical and mental health, physical health, and complete restoration.

WILL GOD HEAL UNSAVED PEOPLE?

Jesus never turned away anyone who came to him for healing. He never said, "You're not Jewish so I can't heal you," or "You don't believe I'm the Son of God." He always healed them, regardless of their condition. But he did expect them to live differently from then on. He expected a heart change to occur. Jesus rebuked entire cities because he did miracles there but they did not repent.[4]

After someone has encountered God in some miraculous way, such as through healing, that person is at a crossroads. God demands an answer to His miracle: "I have just met you where you are. Will you now draw closer to Me?" This is why God will do miracles for His lost children. His heart of love groans with desire for them. This is why God sent His Son to die for all of us, though we didn't know Him or love Him. He reaches down to us in our darkness and lifts us out long enough to see clearly. Then He says, "Do you want to stay here with Me, or do you want to return to your darkness and deception?" Encountering God brings people to a point of decision. This is why some people in strong deception hate the presence of God. Deep down, they know they are against God and they don't want any kind of encounter that demands such a decision. But most people are searching, and very few will ever turn down a radical encounter with God.

I love to see God do supernatural signs, wonders and miracles (whether through me or through others around me). I'm not afraid of Christians who may say, "You have to seek the miracle-*giver*, not the miracle!" I used to languish in that miserable covering as an excuse for why I didn't see miracles. Now, I realize that whenever I see a miracle, I *am* seeing the miracle-giver! I see a part of His face every time I see a supernatural miracle. I see God's tangible, manifest love when I see someone get healed of a sickness or disease that has been plaguing them. And let me tell you, God's face is beautiful, kind, loving, giving, and gentle.

THERE IS NO FORMULA FOR HEALING

Jesus often healed people in different ways. Sometimes it was with a word or a command. Other times it was through a physical act (spitting into some dirt and putting the mud into a blind man's eyes). Sometimes He never even spoke to or touched a person, such as the case of the woman with the issue of bleeding who knew she would be healed if she could only touch the hem of his garment. He told her, "Your faith has made you whole." Healings occurred differently every time. You can't find a formula for healing in the miracles of Jesus. So you have to look one level deeper: how did Jesus know what to do each time?

Jesus said, "I only do what I see my Father in heaven doing." Learn to ask the Holy Spirit how the person will be healed. Is it through a physical action? Is it through spoken words? Is there a sin or unforgiveness issue the person needs to address first?

Sometimes sin or unforgiveness can block the healing from happening. This is where you need to ask the person if they know of any sinful habits, mindsets, or unforgiveness issues they need to address. And, of course, you need to treat the person with compassion, love and honor. You are not there to condemn. You are there as an "ambassador of reconciliation," to restore the person to their rightful destiny in God's kingdom. By addressing the sin or unforgiveness issue, you are helping them become restored which will then result in a physical manifestation of healing.

In the previous example of a person with sin or unforgiveness, you should then continue with the physical healing after you have helped the person deal with it. You will first need to help them through the healing of the spirit and/or the soul, then you will be free to release the healing of the body. God wants every person to be healed and restored in their body, soul, and spirit. In fact, the Greek word for salvation is "sozo" which means "complete restoration of the body, soul and spirit; to save, heal, and deliver; to be made whole." God provided salvation for much more than our souls. He wants us to be completely restored.

THE DANCE OF INTIMACY

I have been swing dancing for about ten years. I've enjoyed it greatly because it is great exercise, a fantastic way to meet people and socialize, and because it is a beautiful dance style that requires communication without words.

Swing dancing is a partner dance. When I dance with a girl, I take both of her hands and we begin to move to a basic swing dance pattern. I can then lead her through some very complex dance moves which involve twisting, turning, twirling, hand-changes, and fly-outs. I don't communicate these moves to her verbally. Instead, she must rely on me to signal her with my hands and arms, which is where most of the communication takes place. If she keeps her arms fairly rigid, then she will feel as I begin to pull her into an Inside Turn which causes her to twirl into me. Or she will feel my hand on her shoulder, gently pushing her away from me while I hold her other hand so that she twirls away from me. At all times, she must keep a rigid arm position so she can feel me as I move her in different directions.

With the smallest tug of her arm, or the slightest twist of her wrist, I can direct her into any dance move I want us to make. We become as one through non-verbal communication. Others watching us often wonder how we can move so effortlessly and without any words. How does she know what to do and when? Does she guess? Why doesn't she trip over my feet? How do I manage to never step on her feet? It is because she has learned how to hear the communication of the lead dancer. If she was looking for it in my words, she won't find it. But she knows to find it in my hands. Once she knows how to "hear" me, we can communicate as easily as with words.

You and the Holy Spirit are like dance partners. The Holy Spirit is the "lead dancer," and you are the "follow." Learn to sense what He is doing and in what direction He is moving. This is a learning process. At first, it may take you longer and the results may be messy and ungraceful. But as you continue working with Him, you will become much more experienced and you will learn how to hear His voice without having to consciously think about it. Just like how a couple learning to dance for the first time won't immediately be winning any dance competitions, if they continue at it they will become more skilled. But in your situation, you are teaming up with an expert dancer. This gives you an immediate head start because the Holy Spirit already knows all the right moves. You just need to hold on tightly and feel for the way He's moving. As soon as you feel Him move left, you'll also move left. When you feel Him about to spin you around, you'll be ready to twirl. And then as you continue in this "dance," you'll become so experienced that you can practically anticipate His next move and you'll be ready for it.

A General Model for Healing

The process of releasing God's healing is pretty straightforward:

1. Interview the person – find out what's wrong.
2. Ask the Holy Spirit how this person will be healed.
3. Make declarations by faith.
4. Check the healing progress.
5. Sometimes faith needs an activity.

First, find out what's wrong so you know what kind of healing they need to receive. Then ask the Holy Spirit what needs to happen for the person to be healed. If He isn't giving you any specific direction to move in, then go ahead and make declarations by faith. Command pain and sickness to leave. Release the presence of the

Holy Spirit to flow into their entire body. You don't need to earnestly pray in tongues for 30 minutes. This can quickly lead you into a human striving process. Jesus *already* won the victory over death and disease 2,000 years ago. Now, rather than praying for it, you are simply releasing it through your words of faith. Speak a bold word of faith such as "I command this pain to go" or "Be healed" and watch as God puts His power on your words of faith. When you speak the word(s) of God, He always releases His power on it. God is already speaking those words over people but He is waiting for His saints to listen for His words and to repeat them with their own voice. When God created the universe, He did it with spoken words. He created light with a spoken word. Now, God has given us power on our own words as we make declarations by faith. We certainly don't need to use our words to ask God to do anything because He's standing there in heaven saying, "No, no! Don't ask me! I'm asking you! Just speak the word boldly and watch me put my power on it so it becomes true!"

You are not praying for God to heal them, but there may need to be some communication with God so He can reveal things to you that may be blocking the healing grace from reaching the person. So look to Him during this process. Ask Him questions and seek out the answer. If He doesn't say anything or reveal anything to you, it's probably because you already know what to do. But give Him an opportunity to override what you know. There will be times when the healing will only happen as He leads and guides you through a process of revelation.

When you are making declarations of faith, speak life and health into their body, especially the part that needs healing. Because you are speaking the words of God, His grace will be on your words to make them come to pass. God's grace always falls on His words. You already know it is God's will to bring healing, so you know you are speaking His words through your faith. You also know you have been given authority over sickness, disease, pain, and even death. So do it confidently! Expect a healing to occur.

Ask the person if they feel any different. You need feedback to know whether they're now totally healed or only partially healed.

Finally, remember that sometimes faith needs an activity. Peter and John told a beggar to "Rise up and walk." But he wasn't healed until he took Peter's outstretched hand so that he could be helped up onto his feet. At that instant, the man's feet and ankles became strong. Many healings need an activity of faith. Don't be afraid to ask somebody to try doing something they couldn't do before. But be careful to do it in a safe and honoring way!

How To Check Progress of the Healing

Ask the person if they notice a difference from before. After Jesus spit on a blind man's eyes and put his hands on him, He asked, "Do you see anything?" (Mark 8:23) He needed a progress update to know if further healing was required or if it was complete. Many times, a healing is only partial and you need to continue releasing it until it reaches 100%.

If you're praying a healing that is easily measured such as bad eyesight or pain that they had currently been experiencing, ask them to give you a percentage of the healing progress. For example, is it now 10% better or 80%?

If you see only a partial healing, keep praying and releasing the healing until it reaches 100%. Jesus did this in Mark 8:22-25.

> *They came to Bethsaida, and some people brought a blind man and begged Jesus to touch him. He took the blind man by the hand and led him outside the village. When he had spit on the man's eyes and put his hands on him, Jesus asked, "Do you see anything?" He looked up and said, "I see people; they look like trees walking around." Once more Jesus put his hands on the man's eyes. Then his*

eyes were opened, his sight was restored, and he saw everything clearly.

If Jesus had to pray for somebody twice, I don't mind pressing in for someone's healing repeatedly. In fact, I've seen people get a complete healing after praying seven or eight times! I can't explain it but if it worked for Jesus then it works for me.

When you're releasing healing for pain, sickness or disease, sometimes the Holy Spirit will allow the person to experience a physical sensation to let them know they're being healed, such as:

- Heat sensation
- Tingling sensation
- Cold sensation
- Physical sense of the Holy Spirit on them that wasn't there before prayer

I prayed for a woman named Kathy whose kidneys were slowly dying. At the time I prayed for her, her kidney function was around 15% or 20% capacity and was dropping to 0%. At that point, she would need kidney dialysis to filter her blood. But as a result of her kidney failure, already the toxins were building up in her bloodstream because her kidneys weren't able to filter properly. The toxin build-up weakened her physically so that she was almost completely bed-ridden. She was so weak, she could only get up and move around for about 15 minutes at a time. She said her greatest desire was to cook a meal for her family, something she had always enjoyed doing and which she greatly missed.

I asked if I could pray for her and she agreed. I put my hands on her shoulder and invited the Holy Spirit to come and fill her body. I didn't even say or pray anything related to her kidneys, I just released more of the presence of God into her to bring restoration and healing. After about a minute of this, she suddenly jerked and uttered a yelp. Then, she jerked and yelped two more times quickly. I stopped praying and looked at her. She was looking at me with a strange expression so I asked her what had just happened. I didn't know if it was good or bad which is why I was asking.

She said, "When you were praying, I suddenly felt three sharp pains in my kidneys and then I felt the pain physically leave my body! My kidneys are healed now!"

She got a sign of the healing in her kidneys. The sign came in the form of a physical sensation in her kidney area, and she felt the pain physically leave her body so that she knew her kidneys were healed by God.

A month later, she had a kidney test that showed her kidneys were now getting *better!* Her doctor said that wasn't possible. Once they start to degrade, especially to this degree, they don't get better. Then about six months later, she had another kidney test that showed they were getting significantly better. But she saw her own results immediately after the healing. Where she had been virtually bed-ridden before, she now had strength in her body for the first time. She was able to cook meals for her family, clean her home, run errands, all the things she had been wanting to do. And even more amazing, I later found out that she joined a bi-weekly water aerobics class to help regain her strength and to increase her stamina further! She was a walking miracle.

You will notice that sometimes there will be a physical manifestation of the healing, such as heat or electricity. Always ask the person, "How do you feel right now?" and let them describe it. Don't ask, "Is the pain gone?" or they may feel pressured to say yes.

If you ask the person how they feel, and they say the the pain moved to a different part of their body during or after prayer, it may be a spirit of affliction requiring deliverance. I've never come across this yet but I've heard others say that they encounter this issue occasionally. Just take authority over the spirit and command it to leave. You have the authority and it has no legal right to be there (unless the

Holy Spirit is showing you otherwise). So command it to leave, then ask the person what they feel. Let them describe the results.

Sometimes there may be a legal reason why the pain, sickness, disease, or spirit of affliction is there. Legal reasons could be things like unforgiveness, witchcraft, or believing a lie. You can ask the person about these things. Or you can use the gift of discernment and the gift of prophecy to allow the Holy Spirit to reveal these things to you. Either way, talk about this with the person in a way that is helpful and loving. You don't want to bring shame; they're here for healing, not judgment.

God wants to extend His mercy and healing to them so deal with their hearts carefully and with honor. Help them through the process, including (if necessary) having them repeat after you as you lead them through a prayer of repentance. If they were involved in witchcraft, you can have them repent for it and renounce it. Or perhaps they were the recipient of a curse which means you'll need to command the curse to be broken. After trying these things, ask the Holy Spirit if that's all. He may reveal something further that needs to be dealt with.

If the Holy Spirit isn't revealing something to you and you seem to be coming up blank, ask the person you're praying for to do this part for you. Have them to close their eyes and ask the Holy Spirit to show *them* what may be blocking or hindering the healing that Jesus has for them. Then ask them to tell you the first thing that pops into their mind. They may need a bit of coaxing since they'll think they imagined it, but almost every time it will lead you both to the answer.

SOMETIMES FAITH NEEDS AN ACTIVITY

If the person you just prayed for had a sprained ankle that was in pain before, you can ask them how it is. Regardless of what they say, have them try putting some weight on their ankle. By doing this, you're giving their faith an activity. Faith without works is dead, just like faith without an action isn't faith… it's only a feeling. Many get their healing while they're testing it out, rather than during the prayer.

Jesus did this many times such as when he healed ten lepers by telling them, "Go show yourselves to the priests." And *as they went*, they were cleansed.[5] And when he met the paralyzed man at the Pool of Bethesda, he said, "Get up! Pick up your mat and walk." At once the man was cured. He picked up his mat and walked.[6] He had to at least *try* to get up. He could have just laid there and said, "What do you mean, get up? I'm paralyzed!" But he had faith and he tried. In that brief moment of trying, the miracle occurred because he put his faith into action.

Often, the person will be healed as they are doing the action. Obviously, use care. If the person is on crutches, don't ask them to throw the crutches away only to have them fall and injure themselves further. But find a way for them to take one step outside their comfort zone so they are operating in the realm of faith. In the case of a person on crutches, perhaps because of a sprained ankle or a broken leg, ask if they can lean on you as you lead them through a few steps. Or if the person you just prayed for has bone spurs on the bottom of their foot, ask them to try putting a little more weight on their foot than usual. Remember, the realm of miracles exists just outside people's comfort zones.

For other mobility problems such as arm pain, wrist pain, shoulder injury, or back pain, have the person try something they couldn't do before. If they had knee pain, ask if they want to try doing a few knee bends or walk up and down some stairs. I can't count the number of people who've been healed of knee pain by a simple declaration of faith and then having them test it out! If you've never seen someone healed of mobility problems such as these, you may be surprised by how easy it is to release God's healing. I often rejoice and shout as much as the person who was just healed when we both see their progress while they're testing out the miracle.

YOU AND THE HOLY SPIRIT ARE PARTNERS

Jesus only did what He saw the Father doing in heaven, so He always had the perfect model for how to get people healed. I believe many of the times where we don't see an immediate healing result, it is usually because we haven't learned to hear the Holy Spirit speak the solution or strategy to us. This is where the gift of prophecy fits perfectly with the gift of healing.

As God speaks to you through the gift of prophecy, you'll begin to see or sense what needs to happen for the healing to occur. Maybe the person needs to be delivered of a demon or perhaps they are believing a lie that is preventing the healing from occurring. Maybe there is a prophetic act that needs to be done for the healing to occur. You will only know these unique strategies as you ask the Holy Spirit every time, "What do you want me to do so that this person can be healed?" Then listen with your spirit.

By becoming skilled at the gift of prophecy so that you can see and sense things by the Holy Spirit, you will be open to hearing His answers to this question. This is how Jesus knew to spit on a blind man's eyes. Jesus didn't question it, He just did what the Holy Spirit showed Him to do. Physical obedience always brings spiritual release.

I was on a mission trip in Tepic, Mexico where our team saw about 95% of the people we prayed for completely healed. But in one specific case, a couple of people were praying for a woman who had been experiencing terrible pain in all of her joints for the past 11 months. I had just finished up with someone else who was healed so I was looking for another person to pray for. I joined this team and asked them what was going on.

One of them replied that they'd been commanding the pain to leave and releasing God's healing and His presence, but there was still absolutely no change. That was pretty amazing considering how quickly people got healed of pain like this the other times we prayed for them! So I asked the Holy Spirit what we needed to do. He replied by prophetically showing me scaly, pockmarked dinosaur skin on the woman's back for a brief instant. I saw this in my spirit, through my imagination. I asked the Holy Spirit what that meant. He said, "Something in the environment around where she lives has been bad for her." I wondered if it was a bad *spiritual* environment or a bad *physical* environment. The Holy Spirit didn't reply, so I asked the woman through the translator. She replied that she had lived in a bad physical environment. I asked the Holy Spirit what we should do next. He immediately showed me a picture of a waterfall above her head with the water pouring down over her. I told the other two team members to put their hands above her head and to release the cleansing water of God over her and through her. We all put our hands above her and released. As we did this, I could see in my spirit that the water was flowing down from our hands and wasn't just washing over her body, it was actually flowing internally through her body and cleansing her from toxins. After 30 or 40 seconds, I could sense that she was totally clean. I asked her how she felt. She said she felt absolutely amazing! She felt like a different woman. We asked her to try doing some knee bends and see if there was any difference. She did 5 or 6 knee bends and said there was no more pain. So we asked her to go up and down some nearby stairs. She did so and she was getting more and more excited by the second as she realized the extent of her healing. She was completely pain-free in all her joints!

You are the Holy Spirit's partner. You are His resource by being His mouthpiece in the physical realm as His Spirit occupies your body. But He is also your partner. He is there to reveal truth to you, to give you strategies, to give you wisdom, revelation, and insight for what needs to happen. Continue pursuing His voice through the gift of prophecy until you can always hear the strategies at times when people don't seem to be responding to the Holy Spirit's healing.

Another Example of Partnering with the Holy Spirit

After service one day, a woman came up to me on the prayer line and said she got hives on her arms every time she came to church. It started a few months prior and it was really bothering her. Even as she was telling me this, she was scratching her arms. I knew immediately that her hives were most likely caused by something spiritual as opposed to something physical or medical. She couldn't think of any reason why she suddenly got this problem a few months earlier so I asked the Holy Spirit to show me what the cause might be.

He showed me a brief image of a big black umbrella over her head. I asked the Holy Spirit if it was a good umbrella or a bad one. He allowed me to sense that it was bad.

I didn't know why an umbrella might be bad. So I asked Him why. He showed me the umbrella again and this time I saw rain coming down on it and splashing over the side of the umbrella so that the woman didn't get wet. I figured that if the umbrella was bad then the rain must be good. And if the rain was good then it was bad that she wasn't getting it. So I realized the rain represented the presence of God. Something was blocking her from it.

I asked her if she could experience the presence of God. She said no, not for many years.

I asked the Holy Spirit what the black umbrella was. He didn't tell me. I told this privately to my prayer team partner who was standing next to me. She told the woman we were praying for to ask the Holy Spirit what was blocking the presence of God in her life. The woman thought about it for a moment and then said, "I don't know if this is me or God because it feels like it's just me. But I heard the word 'witchcraft.'"

My prayer team partner asked her, "Were you involved in witchcraft in the past?"

The woman replied, "Yes, about 8 or 10 years ago."

"Did you repent of that activity and have God remove its effects from you?"

"No," the woman said. "Not yet. I haven't participated in witchcraft in many years but I guess I never repented and got cleaned up from it."

So we led her through a simple prayer of repentance and we broke off the spiritual ties that might still be lingering. We broke off any curses that may have still been on her. Then we released the presence of God to fill every part of her where the witchcraft and evil spirits had been hiding.

We asked if she could feel the presence of God. When she closed her eyes, was she able to see Jesus?

She said she could feel and see (in her spirit) a bright light. She could almost make out the face of Jesus. She could definitely feel His presence in her for the first time in years.

Her hives also disappeared and she had stopped scratching her arms at this point.

The Holy Spirit revealed to all three of us the strategy that we needed to not only bring healing to her body, but to also bring her into a more intimate encounter with Jesus. The hives were nothing more than a symptom of a spiritual disease that was robbing her from the face of Jesus and from physical health. Through these revelations and the breaking off of witchcraft, she received even more than she expected.

REASONS WE MAY NOT SEE IMMEDIATE RESULTS

Why do we sometimes not see immediate results when we release healing into someone? There are many possible reasons.

Most importantly, there is a difference between a healing and a miracle. All healings are miraculous, of course, because they're from God. But a miracle occurs instantly while a healing can take a little time. Remember the story of the ten lepers in Luke chapter 17 who shouted to Jesus, asking Him to have pity on them? He simply told them, "Go show yourselves to the priests." As they went to the priests, they were healed. The healing didn't happen the moment Jesus said the words. It happened as they put their faith into action.

As you're looking for people to whom you can give healing, you may not always hear back from them when they go home and realize they've been healed. You may have spent an hour with them, pushing for the full healing and maybe seeing little or nothing. But, like in the case of the lepers, it may be "as they're going" that they're healed. Out of those ten, one of the lepers came back to thank Him for the healing.

Whether or not we hear back from everybody about the results of a healing encounter, we must still push forward. We must always believe that God is good, that He is our healer, and that we have been given the gift of healing.

We may not see immediate results because we need a revelation from the Holy Spirit as to what may be blocking this particular healing. Ask for strategies and let Him show you in your imagination.

Until we see miracles, signs and wonders on the same scale (or rather, on a greater scale) than the life of Jesus, we must pursue more anointing, power, presence and purity. These will allow us to minister in greater supernatural power.

We need to increase our faith through prayer, fasting, and intimacy with Jesus. Our fruitfulness in ministry flows from our intimacy with Jesus.

Sometimes, the only way we're going to see someone get healed is when we contend for the healing. Contending is simply pushing forward until we see the expected result. We don't let frustration, doubt or fear get in our way. We push past that and press on until we see success. To many, this will look like incredible faith. But really, it's very practical. Do you believe that God wants to heal the person? Yes, you do. Are you going to stick it out until the forces of hell relinquish their prisoners, allowing you to bring them into their rightful freedom through the name of Jesus? Yes, of course!

Hebrews 11:6 says, "Without faith it is impossible to please Him, for he who comes to God must believe that He is, and that He is a rewarder of those who diligently seek Him." (NKJV)

Through our radical faith, we must diligently seek the healing miracle we know we have access to. We cannot stop until we are able to release it to the person in need. God always rewards those who diligently seek Him and His kingdom. Diligence is faith in action.

The healing you're going after may require diligence. Take time to pursue the healing with passion and faith, remembering that God always wants to heal everyone.

In 1 Kings chapter 18, verses 41 through 45, Elijah was praying for rain. He kept sending his servant to go look toward the sea and return to tell him what he saw. Six times, the servant returned and told Elijah that nothing was there.

On the seventh time, the servant returned and said, "A cloud as small as a man's hand is rising from the sea."

Elijah knew that this small cloud was going to be a torrential downpour on the famine-stricken land. He knew it was going to come. He didn't grow so frustrated and embarassed after sending his servant five or six times that he finally gave up and went home. He diligently pushed forward until it happened. Because he *knew* it was going to happen. Maybe you think that's great faith. I think it was just righteous stubbornness. When we put faith on a great pedestal, sometimes we put it so high that it becomes unattainable.

When I put myself in Elijah's situation, I imagine myself being stubborn and not giving up until it rained. I imagine telling God, "Look, I'm not going home until it rains. Whether that's a month from now or five minutes from now makes no difference to me. It *will* rain."

Sometimes, a person's healing may start small and grow as you believe and contend for it. Maybe you released healing on someone, then asked them to check it out and find out what God had just done. They may say it's only 5% better. Right there, you know you've seen the hand of God moving in their life. That 5% is miraculous! Rather than focus on the 95% that didn't change, we must choose to give thanks and glory to God for the miraculous 5% that *was* changed.

Jesus showed us that thankfulness produces increase when he thanked God for the five loaves and two fish. His thankfulness caused a supernatural increase so that it multiplied into enough food for thousands!

Jesus recognized that the small amount of food that was available was provided by God, but it was an invitation to a far greater miracle. Jesus had to jump over a hurdle by His faith. The disciples saw what they didn't have, but Jesus saw what God had provided and knew that God would provide more.

Many times, it's the same thing with healings. It may start small but requires faith to bring it all the way to 100%.

Isaiah 9:7 says, "Of the *increase* of his government ... there will be no end." The kingdom of heaven always wants to increase. God is looking for men and women of faith (or divine stubbornness) who won't give up until they have seen the kingdom expand into people's lives. With this kind of faith, you're going to see healing miracles occur through you on a scale you could never imagine.

Don't be afraid to pray again

If you have asked someone to pray for your healing, be honest about the progress. If you cannot discern any difference from before, don't be afraid to say it. When you're under the "spotlight" of attention from others who are praying for you, it can feel uncomfortable and you don't want to let them down.

Remember, you're in a safe culture where honesty and honor prevail. Allow yourself to be loved by remaining there and letting them continue to release healing into you. If you feel a lot of pressure to tell them the progress is better than it really is, or if you feel uncomfortable receiving more prayer or "taking up too much of their time", that is a strong sign of insecurity.

I don't say this to condemn you but to challenge you to push past it! You are worthy of the prayer team's time. You do deserve to be loved and served. At that moment, your mindset may be pushing you to leave the place of healing (i.e., return to your seat if you're at church) because of insecurities or feelings of inadequacy or unworthiness. Remind yourself that you do deserve to receive this healing because Jesus went through an awful lot of work to get it for you. You do deserve to receive continued prayer and release of the kingdom by one or more people, even if it takes several hours. If they want to keep praying, let them!

Or if you want them to keep praying but you can see that perhaps they're becoming a bit frustrated, speak out your faith! Tell them you believe you'll be healed and you need their help. Be passionate and dream out loud. Fill them with the same faith and passion that you have for your healing and they will immediately respond. Whatever you do, do it with passion and with a radical expression of faith.

Likewise, if you are praying for someone (whether they're a believer or not), don't be afraid to ask them if you can continue ministering to them. You know that the kingdom of God grows, increases and advances which can take some time. Communicate with the other person. Teach them this if they need to know it, or simply ask if you can continue to pray and minister to them. Definitely be considerate of their time constraints, but be bold in your communication. You are the minister. You know what needs to happen. So be a bold leader.

A few years ago at a Bethel Church conference, there was a man who was praying for a woman who was blind. He started praying for her during a morning session around 9 or 10 o'clock. She didn't seem to have any response after a few minutes of praying. Most people would stop there, thinking, "Well, she probably wants to get back to the conference and obviously I'm not making any progress so I don't want to waste her time or mine." Well this guy was determined to see her healed. He knew God could do it. He was tired of not seeing this kind of healing. He decided to put God to the test (in a good way) by not stopping until it happened. He didn't care how long it took or what he had to do. He could see this woman wanted to be healed and he wanted to give her the miracle she was contending for. So he decided he would stay with her and continue praying for as long as it took. She was okay with that so he prayed for her all day. In fact, he never left her for 12 hours. For 12 straight hours, this man continued releasing the kingdom of God into the woman's blind eyes until finally, later that evening, her eyes opened up and she could see!

This is radical faith. This is contending for a miracle. And this is determination. He sought after a breakthrough and didn't let time stop him. He didn't let doubt or insecurities stop him. He knew that her healing was more important to her, and to him, than the conference. He chose to sacrifice his own time and comfort for another member of the body of Christ. God honored his faith and compassion which resulted in an awesome breakthrough.

---

[1] Matthew 6:10
[2] Matthew 28:18-19
[3] Paraphrase of 1 John 4:4
[4] Matthew 11:20
[5] Luke 17:14
[6] John 5:8-9

Chapter 11

Now Go!

This book is not intended to be merely informative. Information must be experienced and tried so that it becomes a part of your experiences rather than a list of facts. My primary purpose is to equip, empower and encourage you to take a risk, try these things out, and encounter the truth of this information. Once you see that this works, that God really does want to do supernatural things through you, and you see it happening in your life as you take risks, then you will start living your supernatural destiny.

A Christian without a supernatural lifestyle is like a fire without heat. If Jesus never did miracles, we would never have believed He was sent by the Father. We call ourselves Christians because we pattern our lives after Christ. This includes the supernatural activation of our faith being acted out in miracles, signs and wonders. We can and should manifest God's kingdom on earth. We can do His will by allowing the Holy Spirit to do miraculous things through us, to bring divine justice by restoring blessings that have been stolen by the enemy.

The only reason I've seen such incredible results in so short a time is because of a few essential things: 1) I know my identity and authority as a son of God, 2) I believe I can do it, 3) I take risks that put my faith into action. That's it! I step out in faith and God does the rest. He honors my faith as He performs miracles through me.

I find it interesting that when Jesus ascended into heaven, the disciples stood there staring intently up in the sky in awe. He had just given them His authority as well as the Great Commission which can be summarized as: "Now go!" As the disciples stared skyward, some angels appeared next to them and said, "Why do you stand there staring up into the sky? The same way you saw him leave you will also see him return."[1] The angels gave the disciples a gentle rebuke by reminding them that they had a mission to accomplish. They weren't supposed to stand around waiting for Jesus to return. They were to *GO!*

Many Christians today are waiting for something. They're waiting for His return. They're waiting for the next revelation. They're waiting for more faith or more power. They're waiting for revival. We should eagerly anticipate every one of these things. But we shouldn't put the Great Commission on hold while we wait. He has given us a mission. He knew we couldn't accomplish that mission without supernatural help, so He sent us the Holy Spirit to dwell in us and allow us to walk in Christ-likeness. We are now filled with the exact same Holy Spirit who dwelled in Jesus and allowed Him to walk a supernatural, miraculous life. What an exciting thought!

The only reason you're reading this book is because—deep down—you yearn to live in the fullness of the destiny into which God has called you. You're now equipped with enough information to get started, but the rest is up to you. I encourage you to take risks. Experiment. Try things out. If you don't seem to have success, don't worry and don't stop. Remember that God rewards risk, not success. Risk requires faith and that is what God honors in you. Keep pushing into the miraculous lifestyle that God has for you and you will definitely see stunning results. God has promised this destiny to you. You are worthy because you are a son or daughter of God and He honors your faith.

I'd like to leave you with a final testimony. This is more than a testimony of healing; it's a testimony of a changed identity. Once I understood my identity in God, I began to naturally live a supernatural life. You can too. I hope this story underscores the importance of everything you've read in this book. I hope you are inspired by my own radical change. If I can do it, I know you can do it.

"I'M A REVIVALIST, I'VE GOT TO DO SOMETHING!"

Recently, I was participating in a business conference call. There were six people on the call; three from my company and three with our client company.

As we got started with the call, my partner begins by asking Laurie, a woman working for our client company, how her back was doing. Obviously, he was familiar with her situation and was asking for an update. I, on the other hand, knew nothing about this situation. In fact, I had never spoken to Laurie before. She answered my business partner's question and I expected it to be a 15 or 20 second response. When somebody asks you, "Hey, how you doing?" you don't typically go into every single detail of your life. But Laurie went into great detail for about three or four minutes straight.

Keep in mind that I'm not exactly supposed to participate in this call. I'm the programmer. When it comes to this kind of conference call, my job is to just sit there quietly and listen. If I hear a technical question, I can jump in and answer it. If my partner thinks I can add something useful without confusing anybody, he'll toss me a softball question to tell me it's okay to talk about something. But essentially, I'm just there to listen to their needs so I can design our software better.

As Laurie goes into the second and third minutes of detail, I was becoming amazed at her situation. She wasn't just having back pain, she was having *serious* back problems. She said a disk in her spine was herniated. I didn't really understand what that meant except I knew it sounded bad so it must be bad. She said that a few years ago, another disk was herniated and she went in for surgery. For the most part, it fixed the problem and her pain level went down. But now, it was back in a different part of her spine and was causing greater problems than the last time. She was losing feeling in her toes and parts of her leg were seriously hurting due to the way the nerves travel up the spinal column.

Laurie was scheduled for a final pre-surgery appointment the following morning. The actual surgery was going to take place within a couple days. Laurie expected to be out of work for eight weeks.

As she's giving all this detail, I could feel something stirring inside me. I had just graduated Second Year of Bethel School of Supernatural Ministry. "I'm a revivalist," I thought. "What am I going to do about this situation?" That question burned in me. "What am I going to do?"

I actually had time to debate with myself both sides of the question, as Laurie went on for several minutes. I thought, "I'm a revivalist. This is what I do. I've got to do something!" But my flesh was saying, "You're in a business conference call. This is the wrong time and place for prayer!" To which my spirit responded, "Come on, you just need 30 seconds to get her healed. *30 seconds!* What's that compared to her eight weeks of recovery time?" And my flesh responded, "You're going to be in the spotlight with people you don't even know and this is going to be really embarassing.

This situation put me outside my comfort zone. My flesh wanted to just sit there quietly and hope she would finish soon so I could forget about it. But my destiny burned inside of me. I'm a revivalist! This is what I was born to do... to walk in the footsteps of Jesus and follow His model to bring Him glory.

Finally, I made my choice. I thought to myself, "Geeez.... I'm a revivalist! I'm going to push all my chips into the center of the table. I know what this is going to cost me in terms of pride and comfort, but it'll be worth it when she's healed and doesn't need to spend eight weeks recovering at home in bed! Thirty seconds of prayer versus eight weeks recovery... I have to put my faith into action to serve her need."

So as Laurie was finishing up, I said, "Excuse me, Laurie... I'm Aaron, the programmer. I'm also a student in ministry school and I just can't let this opportunity pass me by. Can I pray for you to be healed? I've seen so many people healed of back issues that I have complete faith for your healing. This will just take 30 seconds."

The conference line got dead-quiet. For about three seconds, I heard nothing. Then Laurie said, "Uh, sure. Yes, please pray for me."

So I went for it. Granted, it wasn't my most spiritual moment. I felt really "on the spot" and very conscious of the others who were listening in. I tried not to be distracted by what they must be thinking. At this point, I figured I could call it a success if I could just get through 30 seconds.

I didn't pray for Laurie. Instead, I used the authority given to me by Jesus. I commanded all pain in Laurie's body to leave. I commanded her spinal column and the disks to be realigned by the power of Jesus. I invited more of the Holy Spirit's presence into her body, to bring healing and restoration to anything causing problems in her body. I commanded the nerves in her legs and spine to be restored. I released the healing of the blood of Jesus into her. All this took about 30 seconds. I ended with, "Thank you, Jesus. Amen."

Again, another long pause. Then I heard nervous laughter from some of the people on the line. Yeah, two years ago before I came to ministry school, even being a passionate Christian then, I probably would've been one of those people nervously laughing... feeling a little embarassed for the Christian guy who's taking a huge risk and I'd feel glad that I wasn't him. Now I *am* that guy!

I asked Laurie how she felt. She didn't say anything for about four seconds. Then she goes, "Wow... Wow! I feel a lot better! Yeah, I really feel better. I've been in pain all day and now it's gone.

The pain's gone." As I sat alone in my home office, I tried to imagine her moving around and trying it out, tried to imagine the surprised smile on her face as she realized that God had just touched her.

I was relieved that it was over. I was *way* outside my comfort zone and I was just happy that I decided to step outside it. Whatever happened from that point on was in God's hands.

The next morning, I got an email from Laurie. She was on her way to see her doctor for the pre-surgery appointment and asked for continued prayers.

Later that afternoon, I got an email from her co-worker who had also been on the conference line. He said that she went to the doctor and told him she was feeling a lot better. The doctor questioned her for a couple minutes to be sure. Then he decided *not* to do the spinal surgery. He knew how difficult the recuperation would be and he wanted any reason not to do it. She agreed and the surgery was not performed.

I took a big risk because I knew I had something to offer. I was willing to look foolish because of my compassion and faith. God honored my risk and did a miracle.

I encourage you to go take your own risk and see what miracles God will do through you. **Now go!**

---

[1] Acts 1:10-11

About the Author

Aaron McMahon has recently completed three years of training at Bethel School of Supernatural Ministry and is now working with associate pastor Kevin Dedmon at Bethel Church. He occasionally teaches in the school and leads students on ministry trips and mission trips.

In his free time, Aaron enjoys writing, kayaking, international travel (especially Europe), swing dancing, reading fiction and non-fiction, teaching about the kingdom of God, and learning new things.

This is Aaron's first book. Visit his website to learn more about his upcoming books and ministry itinerary:

www.aaronmcmahon.com

Aaron McMahon is available for speaking engagements.

If you have a testimony you would like to share as a result of reading this book, Aaron would love to hear from you! Please email him at: **aaron@aaronmcmahon.com**

HEAL the SICK, RAISE the DEAD, CLEANSE the LEPERS, CAST out DEMONS

Jesus expects every believer to live the commission in Matthew 10:8. He gave us the Holy Spirit so that we could have the power to heal the sick and raise the dead. To live any less than this is to dishonor our destiny and the price that Jesus paid so we could walk in His shoes. He lives in us and His power flows through us. He gave us authority to do things in His name. **It's time to walk in our destiny!**

These Signs Shall Follow will reveal your identity and your authority. You will learn how to pursue God and see His power manifest through you in miracles, signs, and wonders.

This book gives practical insight on acquiring and practicing the gifts of the Spirit, how to get words of knowledge, how to prophesy, and how to heal the sick.

> **These Signs Shall Follow** is both practical instruction and testimonial. The strongest part of the book is that it is not theory: it is a record of the author's personal experience. Aaron McMahon learned to pursue supernatural realities in the context of a Christian community that values risk. He responded well to the truths he had heard and embarked upon a life-changing journey that is available to every believer. I recommend the book and the journey.
>
> **– BILL JOHNSON**
> Senior Pastor – Bethel Church, Redding, CA
> Author of **WHEN HEAVEN INVADES EARTH**

ABOUT the AUTHOR

Aaron McMahon completed three years of training at Bethel School of Supernatural Ministry at Bethel Church in Redding, California. In just a few years, God has transformed his Christian life from "Sunday Christian" into a *supernatural* lifestyle where God confirms His word with signs and wonders.

ISBN 978-0-557-36686-6
51600